Rails Across Ontario

RAILS
ACROSS ONTARIO

EXPLORING ONTARIO'S RAILWAY HERITAGE

RON BROWN

DUNDURN
TORONTO

All photos courtesy of the author unless otherwise noted.

Editor: Britanie Wilson
Design: Jesse Hooper
Printer: Webcom

Library and Archives Canada Cataloguing in Publication

Brown, Ron, 1945-, author
     Rails across Ontario : exploring Ontario's railway heritage / Ron Brown.

Includes bibliographical references and index.
Issued in print and electronic formats.
ISBN 978-1-4597-0753-5 (pbk.).--ISBN 978-1-4597-0754-2 (pdf).--ISBN 978-1-4597-0755-9 (epub)

     1. Railroads--Ontario--History. I. Title.

TF27.O6B76 2013   385.09713   C2013-904120-6
                                            C2013-904121-4

1   2   3   4   5   17   16   15   14   13

We acknowledge the support of the **Canada Council for the Arts** and the **Ontario Arts Council** for our publishing program. We also acknowledge the financial support of the **Government of Canada** through the **Canada Book Fund** and **Livres Canada Books**, and the **Government of Ontario** through the **Ontario Book Publishing Tax Credit** and the **Ontario Media Development Corporation**.

Care has been taken to trace the ownership of copyright material used in this book. The author and the publisher welcome any information enabling them to rectify any references or credits in subsequent editions.

J. Kirk Howard, President

The publisher is not responsible for websites or their content unless they are owned by the publisher.

Printed and bound in Canada.

VISIT US AT
Dundurn.com | *@dundurnpress* | *Facebook.com/dundurnpress* | *Pinterest.com/dundurnpress*

Dundurn	Gazelle Book Services Limited	Dundurn
3 Church Street, Suite 500	White Cross Mills	2250 Military Road
Toronto, Ontario, Canada	High Town, Lancaster, England	Tonawanda, NY
M5E 1M2	L41 4XS	U.S.A. 14150

In memory of Gordon Wagar, 1943–2012,
my travelling buddy of more than forty years,
with whom I shared many an adventure (and occasional misadventure)
while exploring Ontario's forgotten heritage.

CONTENTS

ACKNOWLEDGEMENTS

Research for this work involved the cooperation and support of many individuals. Among them are Michael Morrow of CN Rail in Sault Ste. Marie, for his time and informative tour of the railway's unusual roundhouse; Cody Cuccitti, curator of the Northern Ontario Railroad Museum and Heritage Centre in Capreol, for his insightful tour of the museum's fine collection; and Deneen Perrin, public relations director of the Fairmont Château Laurier in Ottawa, for an inside look at its historic property. Juris Zvidris of the Canadian Railway Historical Association, Toronto and York Division, shared with the author the favourite train-watching spots enjoyed by his fellow members. Conductors and crew of the Ontario Northland Railway's fabled *Northlander* train shared much knowledge about the sights along that historic train route (as well about the politics of the train's cancellation).

Clare and Richard Smirden deserve much credit for their considerable efforts to save and preserve one of the north's finest railway stations, that in Temagami. I would also like to thank Carol Caputo of Algoma Country Tourism, as well as Sudbury Tourism, and Dr. Lynn Pratt of Thunder Bay for their hospitality. I want to acknowledge the important contribution of Mr. George Bryant, who led me to the railway rock etchings beside the tracks near Gravenhurst, and in particular for the research that he submitted. And none of my books would be possible without the patience of my wife, June, through my many and sometimes prolonged absences to travel the length and breadth of this large province in an effort to track the stories of its railway heritage.

Ron Brown, Toronto, January 2013

INTRODUCTION
THE RAILS ARRIVE:
THE GROWTH OF ONTARIO'S RAIL NETWORK

Prior to 1830, travel around what is now Ontario was slow and arduous. Roads, where any existed, were rutted quagmires for much of the year. Stage travel between Montreal and York (now Toronto) could last up to five days. Canals were dug to ease the shipping of produce, but these were restricted to navigable waterways and were seasonal. It was little wonder that the 1830s saw concerted talk of railways.

Trains were up and running in both England and the United States by the 1830s. Canada's first railway was that which, in 1832, linked La Prairie on the St. Lawrence River and St. Jean on the Richelieu — an 18-kilometre year-round route that eliminated what previously was a 120-kilometre journey over water and land. Ontario's first was a horse-drawn portage railway which bypassed the falls and rapids of the Niagara River by connecting Queenston with Chippawa, located above the mighty cataract.

Nearly two decades would pass before Ontario witnessed its first steam train, one that began at a small wooden station on Lake Ontario and made its way to Machell's Corners (later Aurora) in 1853. This was the Ontario, Simcoe, and Huron Railway.

Following that it was open season. New laws such as the Railway Guarantee Act of 1849, the Municipal Corporations Act, and the Mainline Railway Act, also passed in 1849, helped guarantee loans and empowered municipalities to raise money to finance the building of new lines. Within five years construction was under way on the Great Western Railway, an American line linking New York State with Michigan; the Grand Trunk (GT), which would open a line from Montreal through Toronto and on to Sarnia; and the Buffalo, Brantford, and Goderich (later the Erie and Huron) line, which would connect Lake Erie with Lake Huron. The Brockville and Ottawa and the Cobourg and Peterborough Railways also began operating at this time.

Expansion ground to a halt during the American Civil War, but started again in earnest following Confederation in Canada in 1867. By 1910 more than 115 railway charters had been granted in Ontario alone, and the province was nearing a railway saturation point.

With the growth in towns and cities, and more particularly in profitability, rail lines began amalgamating. By 1890 the Grand Trunk had absorbed the Great Western and the Midland Railways and was quickly gobbling up the many resource and branch lines that were responsible for a spider's web of tracks across southern Ontario.

The Canadian Pacific Railway (CPR) was a relative late-comer to southern Ontario's railway landscape. In 1872, the Toronto, Grey and Bruce (later the CPR) began laying tracks that would ultimately connect Owen Sound with Union Station in Toronto. It operated from a terminus at Queens Quay (near the foot of today's Bathurst Street), through Orangeville, to Owen Sound and Teeswater. It was operating by 1873

and became part of the Canadian Pacific Railway (CPR) a decade later.

Another line that was to become part of the CPR was the Credit Valley Railway (CVR), which began running from Parkdale in Toronto to St. Thomas in 1881, with additional branches to Orangeville and Elora.

The 1880s also saw the CPR add to its network the Ontario and Quebec Railway, which would stretch from Montreal through Smiths Falls, Peterborough, and West Toronto Junction. It had originally shared a junction in Perth with the earlier Brockville and Ottawa line. Following the completion of the CPR's Lakeshore line, its yard facilities were relocated to Smiths Falls and all evidence of the yards and buildings in Perth were long gone. In 1883 the Ontario and Quebec (O&Q) acquired the CVR, both of which became part of the CPR the following year.[1]

In 1914, the CPR completed its new Lakeshore Line, which connected with the existing O&Q line at Agincourt and paralleled the tracks of the GT between Bowmanville and Belleville, before meeting the O&Q again at Glen Tay near Smiths Falls. Traffic on the O&Q between Havelock and Perth diminished and the historic old line was finally abandoned between Havelock and Glen Tay between 1971 and 1983.

As the railway network expanded, hubs began evolving in many Ontario towns, largely contributing to the major cities they have become today.

With its location on a large, protected harbour, Toronto began early. The Grand Trunk arrived in 1856 and quickly connected with the Ontario, Simcoe, and Huron Railway, building its first Union Station, a simple wooden structure situated on the shore of the bay.

St. Thomas, a divisional point for the Canada Southern Railway, also attracted the Canada Air Line, a subsidiary of the Great Western, as well the Credit Valley Railway, a part of the CPR network. Stratford, and Palmerston also became hubs for rail lines, which extended out from the central St. Thomas station like spokes of a wheel. Divisional points appeared at 140-kilometre intervals and turned many track-side villages into busy towns and cities.

The Canadian Northern Railway (CNo) was another latecomer to the southern Ontario railway scene. Launched by William Mackenzie and Donald Mann in Manitoba in 1896, their national network arrived in Ontario with lines from Ottawa to Rainy River, from Toronto to Capreol, and from Toronto to Ottawa in 1908. While the northern routes remain used by the CNR, that from Toronto to Ottawa simply triplicated the routes of the CNR and the CPR and was soon abandoned. In fact, in Brighton all three stations were literally within shouting distance of each other.

Meanwhile northern Ontario was opened up with three major east-west lines, namely the National Transcontinental Railway, the Canadian Northern Railway, and the Canadian Pacific Railway, and two north-south lines, the Algoma Central and the Temiskaming and Northern Ontario railways. Here, the CPR was the first line on the scene with the completion of its much-delayed transcontinental route in 1886. In 1908, the Canadian Northern Railway made its way from Capreol through Hornepayne, Nakina, and Port Arthur before exiting the province in Rainy River. Those portions between Pembroke and Capreol and between Longlac and Thunder Bay have been abandoned by the CNR.

The National Transcontinental Railway was the "national dream" of Prime Minister Wilfrid Laurier, with a route that in 1912 connected Quebec City with Prince Rupert, passing through northern Ontario between Cochrane and Sioux Lookout. Sections east of Cochrane and between Kapuskasing and Nakina no longer exist.

The provincially owned Temiskaming and Northern Ontario Railway opened up northeastern Ontario to mining, logging, and farming in 1908, continuing on to Arctic tidewater in Moosonee in 1932. The Algoma Central Railway, launched by Frances Clergue in 1901 to access the iron mines in Wawa, and extended to Hearst in 1914, still operates, now under the ownership of CN Rail, and still offers both passenger and freight service.

The financial needs of the First World War virtually ended railway funding, sending lines like the National Transcontinental Railway, the Canadian

Northern, and the Grand Trunk into bankruptcy, and forcing the federal government to create the Canadian National Railway to take control of the country's bankrupt lines. By 1932, with the opening of the Temiskaming and Northern Ontario (T&NO) extension to Moosonee, railway growth in Ontario had ended.

The arrival of the auto age cut into both passenger and freight business. Highway improvements in the 1950s and 60s accelerated the discontinuation of many railway services and track lifting in the 1970s and 80s brought local rail service to an end. Both the CPR and the CNR abandoned passenger service in the 1970s with VIA Rail Canada taking over the routes. Since then, myopic federal decisions have reduced rail passenger service to a fraction of even that, with one transport minister famously proclaiming that passenger trains were as obsolete as the stage coach.[2]

One of the greatest challenges facing Ontario's railway builders was the daunting coastline of Lake Superior.

In their heyday, Ontario's railways had an enormous impact on the province's landscape. Stations stood prominently in cities, towns, and villages, many sporting the era's most fanciful architecture. Railway landscapes featured grand hotels, roundhouses, coal chutes, and water towers. Railway housing displayed its own distinctive styles. Even entire towns, especially in the forests of northern Ontario, bore the trademark grid street layouts. Special Railway YMCAs appeared in many of the more remote divisional towns.

Recognition of Ontario's railway heritage has been belated. It was not until after the federal government enacted special legislation in 1988 that remaining stations could be protected. Known as the Heritage Railway Station Protection Act, the legislation designated more than three hundred stations across Canada, including more than fifty in Ontario, saving them from demolition or even alteration by the railway companies that owned them. Unless some local initiative ensured their re-use, even those stations so designated were not protected from demolition by neglect or arson. Water towers came tumbling down, and historic roundhouses demolished.

What little railway heritage survives is thanks to many local concerned individuals and volunteer groups. They have worked tirelessly to preserve stations, create railway museums, and start up tour trains. Shortlines have saved many discontinued branch lines, while rail trails now offer hikers and cyclists a chance to venture along the routes that were once the domain of the railways.

This volume therefore guides those who love the railways and the stories they have told to the few surviving relics of our railway era.

— 1 —

THE RAILWAY TOWNS

Each region of Canada presents a different image of its towns and villages. For the Maritimes, that image is one of rocky fishing coves and rustic outports. In Quebec it is the tall silvery spires of the village churches. Across the prairies those spires are replaced by grain elevators, although most have now gone, and in British Columbia the mining boom towns come to mind.

Much of Ontario's early urban landscape was in place before the Great Western Railway sent their surveyors across southern Ontario's countryside. Although the railways did not create the urban pattern as they did across the prairies, they had a profound impact upon it.

Those communities that the rails bypassed stagnated, dwindled, or became ghost towns. Those that the railways blessed with a station attracted key industries and prospered. But the most profoundly affected were the divisional towns, many created from scratch by the railways themselves.

THE DIVISIONAL TOWNS

THE GRAND TRUNK

Besides the line stations at 15-kilometre intervals, the railway had more specialized operational needs. They needed places for the crews to change shifts and rest up; they needed locations where engines could be coaled, watered, and repaired. These were known as divisional points, and one existed roughly every 150 kilometres or so. Roundhouses, coal chutes, crew quarters, and repair shops crowded the smoky yards. These locations also required housing for families as well as bunkhouses for the over-nighting crews. In some locations, Railway YMCAs provided such shelter.

But with the end of the steam era, and the arrival of more sophisticated communications, the need for the divisional points dwindled, and many were closed. Crews were downsized and buildings removed. Tracks were lifted, and some fell silent altogether.

Places like Lindsay and Palmerston became early Grand Trunk railway hubs. Tracks radiated out in several directions: from Lindsay they stretched to Bobcaygeon, Haliburton, and Georgian Bay, and from Palmerston to places like Stratford, Owen Sound, and Kincardine.

Lindsay was thriving before the first tracks of the Midland Railway entered town, as it was a key port on the Trent-Severn Waterway and a bustling mill town as well. Palmerston, on the other hand, grew almost entirely around the new divisional yards.

A visitor to Lindsay could be mistaken in believing that the place had no railway history at all, for no railways remain, nor is any track to be seen. Efforts, however, are underway to create a railway display in the town's Memorial Park.

Palmerston, on the other hand, has quite embraced its railway history: the town has saved some of the old yard tracks for their annual hand-cart races, restored the old wooden Grand Trunk (GT) station, and repaired a historic pedestrian footbridge across the yards.

As the Grand Trunk amalgamated several smaller lines through the 1870s and 80s, it established a key divisional point in Stratford. Here it built a locomotive shop, car shops, repair shops, a roundhouse, a YMCA, and a nursery to supply plants for the hundreds of station gardens. Here too the tracks radiated out to places like Goderich, London, Owen Sound, and Tavistock.

Prior to the arrival of the Shakespearean Festival in the 1950s, the city was utterly dependent upon the railway. While much has been removed since the end of steam, the grand GT station still serves VIA Rail travellers, even as the city deliberates the fate of the massive locomotive shops that stand adjacent to the bustling downtown core. The yards, although reduced, still hold diesel and freight cars for the Goderich and Exeter Railway.

With the opening of the International Bridge over the Niagara River in 1873, the one-time ferry landing of Fort Erie evolved into a major railway town. Both the Grand Trunk and the Michigan Central (MC) Railway established yards in this location and influenced the development of the town, with the main street growing parallel to the tracks. While the MC yards lay adjacent to the main street, those of the GT were located at Amigari, further north. In both cases, tracks still exist, but all the railway structures have gone, save a pair of abandoned shops at the end of Warren Street, where the Niagara Railway Museum houses its growing collection.

The Niagara Falls, which attract multitudes of visitors today, surprisingly were not what drew the rail lines. With the opening of the first suspension bridge by the Great Western (GW) Railway across the gorge in 1853, hotels lined the trackside streets and a business district grew two blocks away. In 1882 the Grand Trunk took over the Great Western and expanded its yards north of Bridge Street.

Today, however, the yard buildings are gone, as are most of the tracks. The large brick GW station, however, remains in use. A second bridge was built beside the GT bridge by the Michigan Central Railway. However, the tracks of that line through the city have been lifted, the bridge is threatened with demolition, and the divisional station for the railway, which stood in the Montrose portion of the city (not far from today's Marineland), has been removed. The commercial core, which evolved near the Great Western station, survives today as the Queen Street business district. A community of former railway employee housing remains north of the former yards.

As a major harbour and provincial capital, the city of Toronto evolved into a series of rail hubs with several yards in a variety of locations. The largest, however, were those of the CPR and GT, located close to the harbour. Roundhouses, car shops, extensive sidings, and a new Union Station dominated the landscape.

But even these extensive facilities proved inadequate for the growing needs of the rail lines, and the auxiliary yards were opened. The Canadian Pacific Railway (CPR) added yards at Lambton, the Canadian Northern (CNo) Railway at Leaside, and the GT at New Toronto and East Toronto, creating new towns around these latter three yards.

West of the city a new town was laid out called New Toronto. Its grid pattern of streets south of the tracks was numbered, rather than named, from 1st Street to 38th. Many industries grew around the yards, while the main commercial core evolved along Lakeshore Boulevard. These facilities today have expanded to include storage and maintenance shops for both VIA Rail and GO Transit. Most of the industries have been replaced by housing.

Many wonder why there is a "Main Street" in Toronto's east end. This too came about when the GT selected a tract of land to create another sea of railway sidings. While it named its yards "York," the town that grew nearby was incorporated as "East Toronto" and the commercial main street became "Main Street." The yards remained in use until the late 1990s when the CN closed them in order for a townhouse complex to develop. Main Street still retains a number of commercial and administrative buildings from those days.

In eastern Ontario, the GT made Brockville and Belleville into major railway divisional towns. Both had an earlier start however — Brockville having been a key port on the St. Lawrence River before becoming the county seat, while Belleville filled a similar role on the Bay of Quinte. Brockville's Manitoba yards were established west and north of the downtown and are much quieter now. A neighbourhood of rail worker's housing is still evident near the site of the yards. The turntable and shops, however, lay on the south side of the tracks a short distance east of the station, close to the CPR's north entrance to the historic Brockville railway tunnel.

Belleville, on the other hand, remains a busy CN yard, although in recent years the CNR removed its historic roundhouse and office. The GT typically placed its tracks and sidings well to the north of what in 1856 was the port of Belleville. Near the station are the standard grid network of streets, which once contained the workers' homes. However, the city grew in the subsequent decades, engulfing the railway area. A few commercial buildings behind the station reflect the tendency of such businesses to locate near the station. The one-time station hotel is now a popular tavern.

THE CANADIAN NORTHERN RAILWAY

One of the last of the rail lines to be built through southern Ontario, the Canadian Northern Railway (CNo) found little land left for their divisional towns, and had to fit into the existing urban fabric. After vacating their flood-prone sidings in the Don Valley beneath the Bloor St. Viaduct, they instead established divisional facilities atop the valley. Beside the Canadian Pacific Railway's Ontario and Quebec

tracks they established facilities that included a roundhouse, sidings, and an engine repair shop.

They then formed the York Land Company and hired the architect Frederick Todd to build a modern town which would later be named Leaside. Unlike the usual grid street pattern, Leaside would boast of curving residential streets. With the CNo's bankruptcy in 1919, Leaside's development stagnated and not until the 1930s did it evolve into one of Toronto's more attractive neighbourhoods. Besides the surviving engine house, the CNo's heritage lingers in the names of the local streets such as Laird, Hanna, and Wicksteed, all named to honour CNo executives.[1]

As the CNo moved eastward, the railway needed another divisional facility and found one in Trenton where it had acquired the Central Ontario Railway (COR). They established their facilities at the west end of the town where the tracks of the COR ran close to the Bay of Quinte. While the grand station has made way for a grocery store parking lot, the roundhouse still survives, now home to a mix of businesses. Its impact on Trenton's urban form, however, was negligible, as it was with the line's next divisional point at Smiths Falls where the station and yards now house a railway museum.

When the Canadian National Railway (CNR) assumed the assets of the CNo in 1923, it reconfigured the tracks at the first divisional point north of Toronto, that in Parry Sound, and it removed all evidence of the 1907 yards, establishing new facilities at South Parry and a new station at a more convenient location.

THE CANADIAN PACIFIC RAILWAY

Canadian Pacific Railway (CPR) divisional towns grew up across its southern Ontario network, although few, except Havelock, had much impact on the evolution of the areas in which they grew.

Smiths Falls was already a busy mill town and lock station on the Trent-Severn Waterway when the CPR extended its Lakeshore line through Smiths Falls in 1908 by acquiring the older route of the Brockville and Ottawa Railway. While the earlier Ontario and Quebec (O&Q) yards in Perth have long gone, the yards in Smiths Falls remain filled with rail cars and grumbling diesel engines, even though the yard shops and roundhouse no

The divisional yard and CPR station in Schreiber still hums with activity.

longer exist. Happily, the station remains and is now a community theatre. A number of former rail workers' boarding houses still line the nearby streets, while a neighbourhood named Atironto was laid out to accommodate the families of the large CPR workforce.

West of Smiths Falls, on the original O&Q line, stood Havelock. The CPR gave it a new station, which was completed in 1929 — a fine brick structure which still stands and now serves as a restaurant. The yards also remain in use, storing mining cars that serve the nephaline syenite mines north of the town.[2]

Although passenger service from Havelock to Toronto ended with the cuts by the Mulroney government in 1990, by 2012 plans were being finalized to restore commuter service along the line. The community retains the appearance of the railway divisional town, with its grid of streets and the main street lining the tracks opposite the yards and station.

Along the CPR's new Lakeshore line, opened in 1912, Trenton served as a key divisional point, although little remains now other than a handful of sidings. Located well to the north of the old port's core, the CPR facilities had minimal impact on Trenton's urban form.

On the CPR's Toronto, Grey and Bruce line to Owen Sound, the CPR established a divisional point at Orangeville. Here the "witch's hat" station and the former dining hall survived well into the 1990s. After the station was relocated to become a restaurant, the former dining hall building burned. The yards, along with a new station, now form part of the Orangeville Brampton Railway, which operates both freight and tour trains.

Deeper into southwestern Ontario, the CPR created divisional points at Galt and Woodstock, where stations and yards remain in use, and in London where the large station has become a Keg restaurant.

The CPR owned many of Ontario's early rail lines, including the short-lived Georgian Bay and Seaboard line. Anxious to capitalize on the growing Great Lakes grain trade, in 1908 the CPR created a link from its Ontario and Quebec (O&Q) route to Georgian Bay via Lindsay. After being denied running rights on the GT to its Midland terminal on Georgian Bay, the CPR created its own terminal. A short distance from Midland, the railway carved out a harbour of its own with stations, grain elevators, and a townsite named Port McNicoll.

Taking advantage of its scenic location, the CPR inaugurated a popular train-boat excursion. Travellers would board the CPR's passenger trains in Toronto and travel to the new port where they would board luxury cruise ships such as the S.S. *Keewatin*. Although the link from Lindsay was gone by the late 1930s, the boat-train excursions continued into the 1960s. Today, however, tracks, trains, and even the grain elevators have long gone and the entire town has begun to take on a tired look — but its future appears ready to become revitalized by resurrecting its railway roots. A proposed new resort-condo development by Skyline Developments would include a replication of the original CPR station, complete with a display of heritage passenger coaches.

But the most prominent feature is the return of the S.S. *Keewatin*. Docked now at the foot of the main street, the massive 1907 Scottish-built liner opened in late 2012 as a museum staffed by dedicated volunteers who continue to improve the vessel. In the townsite itself, a few railway houses yet line the streets, although the once busy commercial core is much quieter now.[3]

In 1908, as the CPR was edging its tracks northward from Toronto to Sudbury, it created a divisional point in Muskoka area, aptly naming it Muskoka Station. Today it goes by MacTier and remains a busy CPR town with a more modern station, a main street, which ends at the tracks, and a small string of workers' housing.

The S.S. Keewatin *is back home again in Port McNicoll where it is a floating museum.*

North of Smiths Falls, Carleton Place too evolved into an important railway centre for the CPR with a roundhouse, engine shop, and stone station. Several key buildings yet remain, including the stone car shops and the roundhouse, which since 1942 have been part of the Canadian Wool Growers' Association, and the stone station, which now houses a variety of tenants.

As the CPR continued its line up the Ottawa Valley it added divisional towns at Chalk River and Mattawa. It is a little hard to imagine railway days in Chalk River, as the station, the yard buildings, and the tracks are now gone, and many of the standard rail workers' homes have been replaced by newer dwellings. Mattawa too bears little resemblance to its former role, although the station has managed to survive.

Next up was North Bay — the CPR considered its proximity to a water supply ideal for establishing a divisional point. Here the town grew along a network of typical railway grid streets, with the main street parallel to the tracks. Of the CPR buildings only the large stone station remains, serving now as a museum.

As the CPR continued building westward, more divisional points appeared at Verner, Sudbury, and Webbwood. Verner has become a busy bedroom community for both North Bay and Sudbury and little evidence of its rail function remains.

Sudbury, on the other hand, grew around its abundant nickel mines with the miners' townsites growing into a single urban entity. The main commercial core of the city grew close to the CPR yards, which remain extensive and busy, although the large office was removed in recent times. No other historic yard structures survive, either. The small brick-on-stone station still serves passengers boarding VIA Rail's *Superior*.

Webbwood died when the steam era ended, for no longer did the CPR require a divisional point close to Sudbury. Today those yards are open ground and no sign remains of the divisional functions. A few railway-era houses and former businesses still line the street beside the track. The main commercial core today lines along Highway 17, a short distance north.

To accommodate what was briefly proposed as the CPR's western "terminal" at Algoma Mills, a railway dock was built and the foundations for a grand Château-style hotel were laid. This route was devised in 1873 by then-prime minister John S. Macdonald after he defeated John A. Macdonald, to replace the latter's grand scheme to link Canada by rail. When John A. was again elected he revived the transcontinental line and scrapped the Algoma Mills terminus. Today, while the stone foundations of the hotel lie scattered among new housing, a commemorative parkette recalls the grand dreams of the railway terminal. Here, there are plaques describing the area's history and the plans for the hotel. A mock-up of railway workers laying track, as well as historic photos, makes this spot interesting to visit. The parkette lies south of Highway 17, east of Blind River. The proposed railway wharf remains and is used for boat launching.

After Macdonald's re-election, the government restored the original west coast plan and construction northwest of Sudbury began. The next divisional point became Cartier, which today retains some divisional functions. Crews still use the 1910 wooden station, and a good sampling of rail workers' homes line the streets east of the station.

Gone, however, are the many yard buildings, such as the roundhouse, water tower, coal chute, and turntable.

Chapleau, on the other hand, remains a significant CPR point. Crew changes occur here, the yards throb with diesels awaiting their orders, and a turntable still guides the engines into their engine house stalls. Lookalike railway housing and boxy two-storey duplexes line the streets behind the modern-era station.

A small parkette in Algoma Mills recalls the railway heritage of what was to have been a major CPR terminal

White River is another of those in-between divisional towns. Like Chapleau, White River was laid out by the CPR in what was then bush land. Sidings were laid, and a large Van Horne-style station built. It was at this station in 1914 that a Canadian army veterinarian named Harry Colebourn met a hunter holding a bear cub whose mother had been killed. Colebourn bought the cub, naming it after his hometown, Winnipeg. As was the practice at the time, the bear became the mascot of Colebourn's regiment in England, where the troops nicknamed the bear "Winnie." With his call to the front, Colebourn donated the bear to the London Zoo, where it became an instant favourite of the children, especially one Christopher Robin Milne, who gave the bear's name to his favourite toy, his pooh bear. Inspired by his son's affection for the animal, his father, book writer A.A. Milne, created the enduring children's classic *Winnie the Pooh*.

While the older station was replaced with a newer structure in the 1940s, the bear returned in different form. In the 1980s the town decided that being the "coldest spot in Canada" was not the image they wanted to portray (in fact, Snag, YT, had recorded Canada's coldest-ever temperature). They decided that Winnie worked better as a town icon, and after some resistance from the Disney Corporation (which had acquired copyright to the Pooh images), placed a statue in their tourist park beside Highway 17. In the tourist office, which was designed to resemble a railway station, there stands a life-sized wood carving based on the iconic photo of Colebourn feeding his bear, as well as an extensive collection of Pooh dolls, mugs, and other memorabilia.

A wood carving of Winnie the Pooh with Major Colebourn features prominently in the White River tourist information centre, the town where Winnie was born.

The old rail workers' homes are being replaced with newer homes, although a few yet survive along the streets closer to the station. In addition to the "boxy" duplexes, there are single dwellings with a more interesting roofline. Few, however, retain their CPR colours.

Farther on is Schreiber. This community, like Chapleau, remains a main CPR crew change point. The station is the third on the site, having replaced an earlier building destroyed by fire. Schreiber began life as Isbester's Landing, one of the five landings that the CPR used in shipping construction material to the remote building sites along Superior's rugged shore. It also proved ideal for a divisional point, and so the railway laid out the town with the usual roundhouse, repair shops, coal chute, and water tower. Along the streets on the south side of the station the CPR built their workers' housing in the identical two-storey duplex style. The main street was placed to the north of the station along with the Railway YMCA.

All yard buildings are gone now, as is the YMCA. Most of the housing remains, as do many of the main street buildings. At the end of the main street is the railway display consisting of a diesel locomotive, baggage car, flat car, and a miniature scale model of the old Railway YMCA.

Thunder Bay became more than a divisional point. It marked the 1874 groundbreaking for the CPR's western portion. Here, near the site of Old Fort William, the CPR created yards beside the first grain elevator, and laid out a typical grid-like

town, Westfort. When the shifting sands of the Kaministiquia River proved troublesome, the CPR moved its port facilities downriver where they opened a new station and new yards. While no yard structures remain at Westfort, save an iron pedestrian bridge over the yards, the neighbourhood retains its historic name as well as the grid street pattern.

Ignace too became a busy divisional town laid out in grid fashion with the standard style of CPR workers' housing. A Railway YMCA provided much-needed accommodation in this remote location with its bitter winters. The wooden station, a storey-and-a-half western pattern, diminutive for a divisional point, survived until the 1990s. The town is a much larger place now thanks to the arrival of the Trans-Canada Highway and most of the early workers' homes have been replaced with more modern dwellings, although a few still stand on Front Street, beside the yards. Today only a few of the sidings remain, now used for storage. Commercial activity has moved to Highway 17, while Front Street, and James Street (once the commercial hub) are largely vacant.

Kenora remains another of the CPR's divisional points with its now enlarged Château-style station still used by CP employees.

While the CPR has managed to retain many of its heritage divisional stations, the same cannot be said of the divisional stations, which fell to the CNR. By 1923, the CNR had taken over both the Canadian Northern Railway and the National

Transcontinental Railway (NTR), and set about replacing a number of their early station buildings.

The National Transcontinental Railway

The tracks of the National Transcontinental (NTR) extended across Ontario's far northern forests. In Cochrane it shared the large brick station with the Temiskaming and Northern Ontario (T&NO). The tracks of the NTR passed by the north side of the station, while those of the T&NO passed by the south. The town was laid out in typical grid fashion with the wide main street ending typically at the tracks near the station. Devastating forest fires raged through town in 1911 and 1914, sparing only the station. By 1990, traffic in Cochrane and Senneterre in Quebec was negligible and the Canadian National Railway (CNR) lifted the tracks of the NTR east of Cochrane.

Trackage, however, does survive between Cochrane and Hearst, the next NTR divisional point west. Hearst, in typical urban railway town fashion, has a main street that parallels the tracks and is organized into a grid network of streets. The original NTR station, with its prominent gable above the second storey, lasted until the 1990s. Although the yards are still active with timber trains from the local mill, only a small waiting room remains to accommodate the passengers on the Algoma Central Railway's local train.

In 1908, the NTR established its next divisional point at a place called Grant, but when the CNR absorbed that line in 1923 it moved the town, literally on a train, a few kilometres west to where the CNR had laid a link with the Canadian Northern (CNo) — a place called Nakina. While most of the early hotels and stores in Nakina have been replaced, the main street with its rail workers' duplexes still ends at the back of the two-storey station, now refurbished to serve as a transportation hub and museum.

Like Nakina, the town of Armstrong remains remote, at the end of Highway 627. Here the rugged main street parallels the tracks, although yard buildings are now gone, as is the CNR's brick two-storey station.

The yards at Sioux Lookout are somewhat busier and the NTR's interesting two-storey Tudor-style station still stands, now part of a downtown revitalization project. Sioux Lookout has fared somewhat better than its divisional cousins to the east, and has grown into a key administrative centre for northwestern Ontario and its remote First Nations communities.

Redditt, the last Ontario divisional point on the National Transcontinental Railway (NTR) before Transcona in Manitoba, has nearly vanished. Gone is the two-storey NTR station, replaced only with a passenger shelter for VIA Rail. The town, which was laid out on a nearby hillside, has diminished and the vast yards are now empty. A portion of the roundhouse, however, is now used by a local industry.

The Canadian Northern Railway

Part of the Canadian Northern Railway's northern link to the Pacific ran through the north end of Algonquin Park. Somewhere in that wilderness the line needed a divisional point. The old sawmill settlement of Brent was chosen, where the railway built a bunkhouse, station, roundhouse, and restaurant. Passenger service ended in the 1960s, and with the arrival of diesel locomotives the divisional functions shrank, although a newer, smaller station and bunkhouse were added.

When the tracks were finally lifted in the 1990s, the place became a quiet cottage community where a number of early railway houses, including the newer bunkhouse, yet survive, as well as the community's iconic general store, now a park outfitter.

When the Canadian Northern (CNo) completed its link between Toronto and its Ottawa Valley line at Capreol, it built a large station and created a key divisional point with a roundhouse and engine shops. While a newer station has replaced the original, a separate facility for VIA Rail was built in the 1970s to resemble a historically styled structure. The YMCA, which offered a warm bed to train crews, no longer stands although the roundhouse can still be found at the north end of the yards, now in industrial use, with its turntable filled in. The railway superintendent's residence now houses the Northern Ontario Railroad Museum.

Foleyet served as the CNo's next divisional town. Its station, which remained into the late 1980s, reflected the CNo pattern — a single-storey with a prominent upper cross-gable. The Canadian National Railway (CNR) never replaced it with a style of their own, ultimately tearing down the aging building. While it remains a CNR town, the divisional facilities are now gone, yet a coal chute remains. Little of the main street retains rail-era structures, although a few early workers' bungalows still line the streets near the yards. The VIA shelter is in current need of updating and repair, but remains in service for passengers.

The CNo created their next divisional point in Hornepayne, and the town remains one of the north's busier CNR towns. While the yards are not as busy as they once were, a new station houses the office and crew of the rail workers and VIA engineers. Sadly, the early station, although a solid brick building and supposedly "protected" by federal legislation, is crumbling into serious disrepair, despite efforts by the CNR to find local interest in restoring this historic structure.

The yards still do contain an unusual example of a "square" roundhouse where, due to the extreme winters, the turntable and engine stall are indoors. In addition, the yards also contain a rare cement coal chute. The railway landscape thus still very much dominates this remote community.

Before the CNR relocated the NTO's divisional point from Grant to Nakina, the CNo's next divisional town was Jellicoe, west of Geraldton. Here the station was a twin to that in Foleyet, though it was gone by the 1960s. A railway boarding house stood in the empty yards at that time. Situated on busy Highway 11, and with its tracks missing, Jellicoe no longer resembles a railway town.

Port Arthur, with its magnificent brick station, was the next major point for the CNo. While the station remains, the rails between Thunder Bay and Longlac were removed, amid considerable objections, during the early years of the twenty-first century.

From Port Arthur, the tracks of the CNo lead west to Rainy River and the Minnesota border. Halfway along this route stands the divisional town of Atikokan. Today, the station and most of its yards have been removed.

The Town of Rainy River happily had the foresight to use a provincial revitalization grant to preserve its CNo brick station, the only surviving CNo divisional station in northern Ontario. The yards, however, see little traffic.

HAWK JUNCTION

When Frances Clergue opened his Algoma Central Railway (ACR) to the iron mines at Wawa, his original terminus was located at Michipicoten Harbour on Lake Superior. Later, as the line was extended to Hearst, the junction of the two sections became the divisional point of Hawk Junction. While a more modern crew quarters has replaced the older bunkhouse, the brick two-storey station still serves travellers bound for the remote camps and resorts which yet line the route. Other yard buildings have gone and the spur to the lake has been lifted, the harbour now resembles a ghost town.

RAILWAY CITY, ST. THOMAS

Like many railway cities, St. Thomas evolved into a major railway hub. This era started with the arrival of the Canada Southern Railway (CASO) in 1873, which selected the site as a divisional point, half-way between Buffalo and Detroit. Here it established a roundhouse, repair shops, a car shop, and one of Ontario longest railway stations. The focus of the town moved from the river where it began to the vicinity of the station and yards. The length of the main street testifies to the development of the commercial district between the two cores. While workers' homes are found to the south of the yards, the more affluent section of town lay to the north, where many grand homes yet stand.

Much survives here, including the massive station, now the North America Railway Hall of Fame; the car shops, which now house the Elgin County Railway Museum; and a preserved switching tower, although, sadly, trains no longer pass this way.

THE GHOST TOWNS

When the rails made their way across the Ontario countryside, many of the early towns and villages that they passed dwindled in importance, losing their businesses to the rail towns. A few shrank to the point where they become ghost towns. Other towns that owed their very existence to the arrival of the rails faced a similar fate when their railway functions ended.

The strongest remaining example is Depot Harbour. Built from scratch by railway magnate John Rudolphus Booth, the place is now reduced to foundations in a forest and the gaunt Roman-like ruins of the large railway roundhouse. When Booth built his line through Algonquin Park in 1895, he rejected a terminus at Parry Sound and opted for a large natural harbour on Parry Island First Nations territory. His new town contained more than one hundred dwellings, hotels, schools, churches, and two large grain elevators. It was, for three decades, Georgian Bay's busiest grain port.

When an ice floe in the park damaged a vital bridge, the government denied the CNR funds for repair, and the grain port was very nearly isolated. After the elevators burned in 1945, its reason to even exist ceased and by the 1950s it was a ghost town. Its buildings were dismantled and moved away. Today, the townsite has reverted to forest which contains extensive foundations and the skeletal shell of the roundhouse.

While there are no ghost towns to match Depot Harbour, many once-busy railway junctions have faded away. Scotia Junction, north Huntsville, marked the junction between Booth's line and the Northern and Northwestern Railway and contained yards, housing, and a station. But when Booth's

line was lifted, and the CNR (then the owner of the NNW) converted to diesel, the village no longer had any reason to exist and so faded away to the handful of structures, some abandoned, which remain today.

Many of the remote section villages along the more distant reaches of the ACR have dwindled, but the two key junctions that the ACR shared with the Canadian Pacific Railway (CPR) and Canadian National Railway (CNR) have become ghost towns: Franz on the CPR and Oba on the CNR, although the latter retains a few residents and a string of aging trackside buildings. (According to Elections Canada statistics, it is the smallest voting district in the country.)

The *Superior*, VIA Rail's service between Sudbury and White River, is described (by this author) as the "ghost town train" owing to the string of now-vanished sawmill towns along its route. Biscotasing and Nicholson contain the most visible legacy, as well as Lochalsh, which was a jumping-off point for the gold fields in the area.

While the CPR was building its tracks along the rugged shore of Lake Superior, it needed many lakeside locations at which to bring in construction material and coal, and one of the busiest was Jackfish on Lake Superior's storm-tossed shores. Along with a fishing fleet it was, into the 1950s, one of that railway's busier shipping points and was even featured on postcards. But with the end of the steam engines, the CPR removed the coal dock, while the arrival of the deadly lamprey eel decimated the fishery and ended Jackfish's days. Finally, with the Trans-Canada Highway giving it a wide berth, it became a ghost town with no permanent population at all.

In 1903, the Temiskaming and Northern Ontario Railway opened the forests of northeastern Ontario to farming, logging, and mining. Many of the towns that the railway created remain, growing or at least maintaining their population. A few have not. Between North Bay and Temagami, the little communities of Tomiko and Redwater have become virtual ghost towns, the former with a handful of residents, the latter with only a few seasonal visitors. North of Cochrane, places like Fraserdale and Coral Rapids are but shadows of their former selves.

WHAT'S IN A NAME

On Canada's prairies, the main railway builders were given a near-carte blanche to come up with place names. Many honoured railway executives, some reflected aboriginal names or geographical features, and others were whimsical, such as the string of towns in southern Saskatchewan named entirely after poets.

Railways were more constrained in Ontario, since most of the towns through which they passed already possessed names. But the railways did manage to get a few of their names on the landscape. Angus, for example, was named after Angus Morrison, a director of the Canadian Northern Railway (CNo), while Armstrong derives from W.C. Hewton Armstrong, who was a key railway financier. The divisional town of Englehart was named to honour Jacob Lewis Englehart, who was chairman of the T&NO from 1906–1921. Engelhart also created the nucleus of Imperial Oil in Petrolia.

Foleyet came about in a rather unusual manner. As a divisional point for the CNo, Donald Mann wanted to name it after Tim Foley, but when told there already was a "Foley," Mann allegedly retorted that "We'll name that place 'Foley' yet." And so it was.

Fraserdale comes from Alan Fraser, resident engineer of the T&NO, while Hickson in southwestern Ontario derives from Joseph Hickson, general manager of the Grand Trunk from 1874–1890. Hillsport honours Arthur Hills, the CNo's general superintendant in eastern Ontario, while Hornepayne was the name of a British railway financier, Robert M. Horne-Payne, president of the British Empire Trading company that advised Mackenzie and Mann of the CNo.

At first named Muskoka Station, when the CPR chose this location as a divisional station it was renamed MacTier after A.D. MacTier, general superintendant of the Canadian Pacific Railway's eastern region. When the CPR built the port of Port McNicoll in 1911 it named the location in honour of David McNicoll, general manager of the CPR. Collingwood Schreiber was the chief engineer of the CPR from 1880–1892, when the divisional point of Schreiber was named for him.

The name of Swastika on the T&NO, although not of railway origin, always raises eyebrows due to its affiliation with the Nazi party of Germany. The name, however, was chosen in 1906 when a pair of lucky prospectors hit a major gold vein and happily named it after the "swastika," a native name and a good-luck symbol. Pressures to rename the town "Winston" during the Second World War were met by local resistance and signs that said "Hitler be damned." They were determined to keep their name, and it stands on the station today.[4]

— 2 —

BRIDGING ONTARIO:
THE RAILWAY BRIDGES

We drive over them and we drive under them, but seldom do we pause to wonder at the engineering marvels that bridges truly are. None are greater feats of engineering than the railway bridges.

Stone arched bridges, devised by early Romans, were among the first to be built for the early railways, some as early as the 1820s in England. In North America, the first arched bridges appeared in 1829 when the Baltimore and Ohio Railroad erected a 280-metre bridge at Gwynns Falls, Maryland. The Starrucca seventeen-arch bridge at Lanesboro, Pennsylvania, measures more than 300 metres (1,040 feet) long and rises 35 metres (100 feet). Completed in 1848, it still stands to this day.

By the time Canada's first rail lines were under construction in the 1850s, a new and sturdier type of bridge had already begun to gain popularity. Stronger and cheaper to build than the stone arch structures were the iron truss bridges, criss-crossing beams of iron and steel that supported the plate girders above them.

But the earliest in Ontario, with its plentiful forests, were the wooden trestle bridges. As most were subsequently filled in or replaced with steel structures, few have survived. In Madawaska a low-level wood trestle carries the former right of way of the Booth railway across the Madawaska River. It dates from the 1890s and is about 100 metres across. A shorter, although no less historic, bridge crosses the Pigeon River in Omemee.

In the Niagara Peninsula, three bridges from the Toronto, Hamilton and Buffalo's Port Maitland branch remain at Elcho and Port Davidson. A mostly wooden trestle carries the right of way of the Grand Trunk across the wide Saugeen River valley in Paisley. Along with a second large trestle they now form part of a rail trail. Also part of a walking trail is the CPR's wooden trestle over the Saugeen River in Durham. Wooden trestles also survive as part of the Georgian Trail, crossing the Beaver River in Thornbury and over the Wye River, adjacent to Sainte-Marie Among the Hurons in Midland.

To accommodate bridges over navigable rivers, the railway engineers devised various types of movable bridges. Originating in France was the "bascule" bridge. Here the span could be lifted high into the air by means of a heavy counterweight on the shore. Occasionally the rivers would be wide enough to require a double-leaf bridge.

Vertical lift bridges would see the entire centre span rise into the air by means of counterweights situated inside steel towers at each end. These proved popular along the Welland Canal. They were, however, limited, owing to the height limits and the cost.

With its varied topography and its long period of bridge building, Ontario can boast of a remarkably varied collection of heritage railway bridges. Many still stand, although regrettably a few are threatened with demolition.

NAPANEE

The only stone arch bridge of any significance is that which crosses the Napanee River in the town of the same name. Built in 1856 by the Grand Trunk Railway, it consists of four elegant stone arches on each end of the picturesque structure, as well as four plate girder spans, which cross the river. It stretches more than 250 metres wide and rises about 40 metres high.

PORT HOPE

Another of Ontario's more significant and photogenic heritage bridges is that in Port Hope. It too was a product of the Grand Trunk (GT) and consists of seventeen stone piers topped by a series of plate girders. Built in 1857, it curves across the wide valley of the Ganaraska River in historic downtown Port Hope. Although its height is a mere 25 metres, its length is nearly half a kilometre.

Almost a half-century later, the Canadian Pacific Railway (CPR) was confronted with the same obstacle and built their Ganaraska Bridge using piers of cement rather than stone. It is located only a few metres north of the old GT bridge. This pair of bridges make for rewarding train watching along the two busy main lines.

A Montreal-bound VIA Rail train crosses the historic Grand Trunk trestle in Port Hope.

TRENTON

Finally opened to boat traffic between Trenton and Georgian Bay in 1920, the Trent-Severn Waterway required the railways to put their best engineers to work to bridge the various sections. To allow boat passage, many of the canal bridges needed to be movable, most being swing bridges.

In Trenton on the Bay of Quinte, the wide Trent River and Canal flows down a shallow valley as it enters Lake Ontario. The Grand Trunk bridge was the first to span the river, and was completed in 1857. With the opening of the Trent-Severn

Waterway, a newer bridge was built, one that had to be high enough to accommodate boat traffic. That of the Canadian Pacific Railway, a short distance downstream, arriving nearly a half century later, is a much grander structure with a string of steel girders resting atop a series of nine concrete piers. Both lie to the north of downtown Trenton, where a low-level swing bridge constructed by the Canadian Northern Railway has since been removed, although the piers remain visible. A former swing bridge at Glen Ross, a short distance north of Trenton, is permanently fixed in the "open" position.

PETERBOROUGH

To cross both the Otonabee River and the Trent-Severn Waterway in Peterborough, the Canadian Pacific Railway (CPR) constructed a series of bridges. That over the canal, a Warren through truss swing bridge was built in 1898. Because trains still use the CPR line to Havelock, the bridge closes when necessary to accommodate the trains. A short distance away, over the Otonabee River, the CPR owns another pair of bridges, also Warren through trusses. Built in 1913, they are connected by a causeway and for a time contained a pedestrian deck.

Near the north end of Peterborough, on the CN's abandoned Lakeview branch, a former Grand Trunk swing bridge, built in 1898, now rests on the bank of the canal. Permanently open, the single span covers 80 metres (217 feet). Further upstream, yet another Grand Trunk bridge now forms part of the Lower Trent Trail.

Between Peterborough and Omemee, the Grand Trunk's Doube's Trestle Bridge, now part of the Kawartha Trans Canada Trail, linking the two towns, soars 29 metres over Buttermilk Creek, its steel girders resting atop a string of nine steel piers. Originally 500 metres long, filling has since reduced that span to 200 metres.

OTTAWA'S ROYAL ALEXANDRA INTERPROVINCIAL BRIDGE[1]

The city's first bridge was that built by the Brockville and Ottawa Railway over the Rideau River in 1855, when the first station was located on Sussex Drive. It stretched more than 110 metres (350 feet) and consisted of four through trusses, which rested on low stone piers. The bridge was removed in 1965, leaving only the stone piers visible in the water.

One of Ottawa's more famous landmarks, as well as its busiest bridge, the Royal Alexandra Interprovincial Bridge, was built in 1898 by the Ottawa and Gatineau Railway, and the Pontiac Pacific Junction Railway (later to become part of the Canadian Pacific Railway), to carry its trains across the Ottawa River. At the time of its opening, the main 170-metre cantilever span was Canada's longest. The overall length stretched more than 560 metres and rises 30 metres above the river. Decks on each side of the main truss also allowed pedestrians and carriage traffic. Improvements to those decks in the 1950s enabled cars to cross as well. After the last trains ran in 1966, with the replacement of Ottawa's Union Station, the bridge became a major automobile bridge, with two decks for cars and a third for pedestrians and cyclists. The structure has no fewer than three heritage plaques, and has been named a National Historic Civil Engineering Site.

The CPR's Prince of Wales bridge was purchased by the City of Ottawa for an extension to its O-Train service.

THE PRINCE OF WALES BRIDGE

Older than the Royal Alexandra Interprovincial Bridge, but now unused, the Prince of Wales bridge was constructed over the Ottawa River between 1878 and 1880 by the Quebec, Montreal, Ottawa, and Occidental Railway, a line which later became part of the Canadian Pacific Railway (CPR). The bridge allowed the CPR to link its Quebec network to its new transcontinental line at Carleton Place. It consists of two sections, one with six truss spans between Lemieux Island and the south bank of the river, the second, north section with seven such spans completing the crossing to the Quebec side. Eleven spans extend 55 metres (165 feet) each, one at 50 metres (145 feet), with the longest being 75 metres (265 feet). After the last train crossed in 2001, the City of Ottawa purchased the bridge, intending to incorporate it into its O-Train route, although by 2012 that had not yet happened.

SMITHS FALLS

One of Ontario's more unusual bridges is that at Smiths Falls. This muscular bascule bridge was constructed over the Rideau Canal in 1915 by the Canadian Northern Railway. Known more technically as a Scherzer rolling lift bridge, it remained in use until 1978, and operated manually for most of that time. In 1983 it became a National Historic Site, and remains in its open position to allow boat traffic using the Rideau Canal to pass beneath.

FITZROY

Yet another stunning interprovincial railway bridge connects Ontario with Quebec, well to the west of Ottawa at Fitzroy. Looking for a straighter route to the west, the Canadian Northern Railway decided to cross the winding Ottawa River into Quebec with a 500-metre (1,600-foot) bridge. The structure comprises five segments, including three plate girders and two through trusses built high enough above the river to allow log drives to pass beneath. The bridge was opened in 1915. A second large bridge at Portage-du-Fort brought the tracks back into Ontario.[2]

SOUTH NATION RIVER

In 1909, the Canadian Northern Railway (CNo) being built from Montreal to Ottawa encountered the South Nation River, a sluggish, wide river that enters the Ottawa River at Jessup's Falls. Because the proposed bridge stood between the Ottawa River and a sawmill, the Department of Public Works stipulated that the spans be 50 metres (150 feet) apart to allow passage of the logs. However, the CNo resisted, insisting that the widest span be only 40 metres (120 feet), to which the department agreed. But the problems didn't end there, as some of the piers weakened and collapsed, blocking shipping in the river. It was discovered that the contractor had been using inferior cement that dissolved in the water. Finally completed in 1909, and rebuilt ten years later, the bridge was nonetheless abandoned completely in 1939. The piers remain visible to this day beside County Road 17 near L'Orignal.[3]

MATTAWA

The 500-metre (1,550-foot) railway bridge that crosses the Ottawa River at Mattawa is not that old, having been completed in 1950 after a new power dam forced the rerouting of the Canadian Pacific Railway's Ottawa River tracks. The rail line is still used to haul lumber from the mills at Temiscaming,

Quebec, to North Bay, although the trackage between Mattawa and Ottawa has been abandoned.

LONDON'S BRIDGES

Far from "falling down," the city of London's CN and Canadian Pacific Railway (CPR) bridges are very much in use. The more interesting of the two is the CPR's triple truss bridge, which crosses the North Thames River in three separate spans, with a fourth over Oxford Street. The through truss spans can be easily viewed from Oxford Street and from the small park on the north side of the street. They remain part of the CPR's southwestern Ontario rail network.

Crossing the south branch of the Thames is CN Rail's single span bridge, and is busy with not only the CN's freights but also the frequent VIA Rail passenger trains that follow its Windsor-Quebec corridor. Its origins date to the building of the Great Western Railway from London to Windsor in 1854. In the case of this more recent bridge, the truss deck rests on concrete piers below the tracks, rather than above, which is more usual. Today's structure is more than 180 metres (560 feet) long and rises 22 metres (70 feet) above the river. This train activity on the bridge can be seen from the banks of the river in Greenside Park.

London also offers an unusual stone arch bridge, which carries CN Rail traffic over Thames Street. Although not large, it retains a date stone engraved as 1889.

ST. MARY'S

With its two historic stations, St. Mary's can also claim two stunning railway bridges. That which crosses the Thames River north of the town centre, known as the "Sarnia Bridge," rests on a string of stone piers and dates from the construction of the Grand Trunk Railway to Sarnia in 1858. Now trackless, it carries the Grand Trunk Trail high above the waters of the river. A second bridge, the "London Bridge," completed a short time earlier to link St. Mary's Junction with London, and still in railway use, crosses the wide valley of Trout Creek, a tributary to the Thames, at the east end of the community, and ends at the 1905 brick station. Stretching more than 1/4 kilometre in length and soaring 30 metres high, its steel girders rest on a series of stone pillars. The sight of passenger or freight trains rumbling high overhead make this one of Ontario's better rail photo opportunities.

THE BRIDGES OF RAILWAY CITY ST. THOMAS

The original bridge over Kettle Creek was built by the American-owned Canada Southern Railway in 1871. The current structure, which stretches more than 1,300 metres and rests on a series of concrete piers, which soar high above the diminutive creek, was added in 1927 by the Michigan Central Railway (MCR), one of the line's many successive owners. Built for two sets of tracks, it was sturdy enough to accommodate two trains at once and remains in solid condition. The latest owner was the Canadian National Railway.

After the CN abandoned the line, the fate of the bridge remained uncertain. Finally, in 2013, the community group "On Track St. Thomas" purchased the structure to create Canada's first "elevated park."

A short distance upstream from the MCR bridge is the CNR bridge. Neither as high or as long as the above structure, it does span the entire width of the valley, with simple deck plate girders resting atop a string of steel pillars. It remains in occasional use by CN Rail and can be seen from Athletic Park on St. George St.

GODERICH

Once considered the largest in its day is the CPR bridge over the Maitland River at Goderich. Built in 1907, with the completion of the Guelph to Goderich Railway, it stretches for nearly half a kilometre, rising more than 15 metres above the river. Seven girder spans rest on seven concrete piers. Closed to trains in 1988, the Menesetung Bridge

now forms part of a popular walking and cycling rail trail from Goderich to Auburn.

HAMILTON'S HAUNTED BRIDGE.

It's not very big, but many claim that the old Great Western Railway bridge on the slopes of the Niagara Escarpment near Dundas, Ontario, close to Hamilton, is haunted. The former right of way of the train line is now abandoned, with a new track a short dance up the slope. It was on the older track that a Great Western passenger train plunged into the deep gully on the night of March 21, 1859, killing five on board. Unbeknownst to the engineer, a heavy storm had washed out a portion of the track, all but invisible in the driving rain and dark.

Paranormal investigators claim to have heard noises in the bushes, photographed "orbs," and seen vague shapes moving along what is now a short rail trail that crosses the old bridge. The trail to the old bridge is situated in Cascade Park on Livingston Avenue in the northern section of Dundas.[4]

THE DESJARDINS BRIDGE DISASTER

An even worse bridge disaster occurred in 1857 when a Great Western Railway passenger train began its approach to the short bridge, which spanned the

Desjardins Canal near Hamilton. As the engine neared the bridge, the wheels derailed and began crashing through the ties until those on the bridge splintered carrying the hapless passengers and crew to an icy death. Fifty-nine souls perished in the calamity. A commission of inquiry concluded that the railway had used inferior wood on the ties and the bridge. While a new bridge has been in service for many years, the abutments of the ill-fated structure remain visible below it on the sides of the cut for the canal.[5]

THE BRIDGES OF THE GRAND

As the name might suggest, the Grand River (and a couple of its tributaries) can boast of some grand historic railway bridges. Some are diminutive, such as the Canadian Pacific Railway (CPR) bridge over the Speed River in Guelph, with just a single plate-girder. But what makes this bridge interesting is that it is shadowed by the Grand Trunk bridge, with its seven stone piers, which crosses high above it. Built in 1857, the Grand Trunk (GT) bridge was wide enough to accommodate double tracks. Only a single track remains, while an abandoned roadway runs beneath it.

Between Breslau and Kitchener, the GT crosses the Grand itself, albeit with a simple girder bridge, more than 130 metres (400 feet) long, resting on concrete piers.

One of the longest of the Grand River bridges is that which the CPR built across the Grand in Galt (now Cambridge). Its seven iron spans, in two sections divided by an island, rest on eight stone piers, five of the spans being truss spans, two of them girder style. The bridge and nearby heritage station, part of the CPR main line to southwest Ontario, see frequent freight trains.

One of the river's more attractive towns is Paris, once a busy railway junction. A short distance north of the town rest the abutments of the early Great Western Railway (GW) bridge. This section of track was bypassed in 1877 when the Grand Trunk Railway (the GW's successor) rerouted its tracks through Brantford and built a new high level bridge within Paris itself. That bridge sees frequent trains, including both the passenger trains of VIA Rail and CN freight trains. It extends 280 metres (760 feet) and rises nearly 30 metres (100 feet) above the river. The Galt to Cambridge Rail Trail passes beneath it and offers views of both bridges.

Within the city of Brantford itself, two old girder bridges over the Grand, abandoned by the railways, have been incorporated into walking trails.

Further southeast in Caledonia, where the river widens, there stretches the form of the Hamilton and Northwestern Railway bridge, a line completed in 1875, although the bridge itself is of more recent vintage. Most of that line has been abandoned over the years, with only the portion between Caledonia and Garnet remaining from where a new spur line serves the industries at Nanticoke. The original Howe truss bridge was replaced in 1953.

Cayuga, the Haldimand County seat, enjoyed two rail lines, the Canada Southern and the Canada Air Line. Both were later taken over by the CNR, which abandoned the lines in the 1980s. The more northerly of the two Grand River bridge structures is not visible from any road, however the more southerly bridge can easily be seen from Highway 3. Both are girder plate bridges resting on a string of concrete piers.

THE BRIDGES OF THE GTA

While most residents of the Greater Toronto Area (GTA) focus on gridlock, they seldom ponder the railway heritage that rises above their vehicles. Throughout the region, several rivers have carved ravines into the land. These gullies proved impediments not only to early road travel, but posed a challenge for the railway builders as well.

Nowhere is that better seen than the bridges of the Don. The Don River, while not a large river, has managed to carve an extensive system of ravines, thanks in large part to an earlier and larger river. In 1888, when the Ontario and Quebec Railway (O&Q), a Canadian Pacific Railway (CPR) line, laid its tracks north of what was then the city limit, it built a series of bridges, one over a small gully that fed into the Don, and two others over the

Don's two main branches. While the former was short, it rose high above the gully, and today rests on a pair of uniquely constructed concrete piers. That over the Don's east branch, however, is not only high, but long as well, and consists of plate girders resting on a string of steel bents. While CPR freights frequently rumble overhead, GO trains fly past beneath it following the line established by the Canadian Northern Railway.

After the O&Q became part of the CPR network, that railway realized they needed a link down the Don Valley itself to Union Station. In 1890 it constructed what is known today as the CPR "Long Bridge." In 1928, the CPR set out to build the current structure, and did so without disrupting service on the earlier bridge. It extends 335 metres across the Don River and the GO Transit rail line, as well as the busy Bayview Extension beside the Don Valley Parkway. The CPR discontinued use of the bridge in the 1990s and, still unused, it is owned by Metrolinx.[6] It is best viewed from the lookout point in the Evergreen Brickworks. The O&Q line also extended westward where a high trestle soars above the Humber River resting on piers of stone and concrete.

Further from the city, the soaring CN trestle over the Credit River near Georgetown dates to 1857, and was known as the Stone Bridge. It has been renovated considerably since then. CN's bridges across Sixteen Mile Creek and Bronte Creek on its Toronto to Hamilton line measure

180 metres (490 feet) and 190 metres (560 feet) respectively.

Further upstream the Credit River's east branch dashes down a steep rocky canyon to where it spills into the west branch, a site known as the Forks of the Credit. Built in 1874, the Credit Valley Railway, which clung to the canyon walls, needed a high-level trestle to cross the forks. Built originally as a wood trestle, the 400-metre- (1,146-foot-) long bridge, now steel, still awes travellers both from high above on the popular Credit Valley Explorer tour train, and from below on the Forks of the Credit Road.

THE WELLAND CANAL'S ECLECTIC BRIDGES

Completed in 1833 from Port Dalhousie on Lake Ontario to Port Colborne on Lake Erie, the Welland Canal offers up a wide variety of railway bridge styles, from bascule, to swing, to vertical lift. Because the canal had to be rebuilt several times to keep up with the demands of ever-larger ships, rail lines had to be rerouted. The current version of the canal was finished in 1932, with a bypass around the city of Welland, which opened in 1973. At that time the rail lines were rerouted into a single tunnel beneath the new bypass.

Still active is the Grand Trunk swing bridge over the ruins of the third canal, near St. Catharines. Built in 1887, the bridge replaced a tunnel beneath the canal that dates back to the 1870s. The bridge has remained stationary since the new fourth canal opened to the west. The bridge is of the camelback truss style, the pivot resting on a limestone out-cropping.

Near the south end of Welland, in a community formerly known as Crowland, a swing bridge still straddles the disused portion of the canal. Although it is gated and rusting, the shortline Trillium Railway still occasionally uses the structure to service local industries. A short distance further south, a still-active vertical lift bridge, also owned by the Trillium Railway, continues to serve an industrial area in Dain City.

To the east of the Welland Canal, the Welland River once formed part of the early canal. In 1910, near the city of Niagara Falls, the Michigan Central Railway built a through truss swing bridge wide enough to accommodate double tracks in order to cross the river. After the line became part of the CPR, the bridge was fixed and one track was removed. Eventually the CPR abandoned the line altogether. The bridge is historically significant in that it contains much of its original machinery

Meanwhile in Port Colborne, a girder span swing bridge carries the abandoned right of way of what began as the Buffalo, Brantford and Goderich Railway across the disused second and third canal, while a vertical lift bridge, similar to the vehicular bridge beside it, that crossed the fourth and current canal, has been removed.

Crossing the twin flight locks in Thorold is a double leaf CN Rail bascule bridge, built in the 1930s with the completion of the third canal. These locks, which carry ships in both directions, represent the three-lock ascent of the Niagara Escarpment. The bridge carries both freight and passenger traffic to Niagara Falls and into the U.S.

THE BRIDGES OF THE NORTHLAND

While the terrain in southern Ontario was gentler and easier for the bridge builders, that in the north was uncompromising. Hard granite peaks, wide chasms, and unforgiving muskeg meant bridge-building challenged the engineers and bridge-builders to create some of the greatest railway bridges ever to appear in Canada.

THE PARRY SOUND HIGH LEVEL TRESTLE

In 1906, the Canadian Pacific Railway (CPR) began work on what would become its new main line from Toronto to Sudbury, where it would link with its existing transcontinental line. The portion from Toronto to MacTier, the divisional point, was straight forward with the only serious bridge being that over the Nottawasaga River at Minesing. But the steep rocky terrain of the Canadian Shield was another matter. Major trestles over the French and Pickerel rivers, and at Pointe-au-Baril, proved enough of a challenge, but it was the massive gap over the mouth of the Seguin River at Parry Sound that presented the strongest challenge. Construction began in 1906, and required 5,000 workers and two years to finally complete the crossing.

The steel beams, atop a string of concrete and steel piers, stretches more than 500 metres wide and rises 35 metres high above the harbour. Trains rumble across the structure at frequent intervals and include VIA Rail's westbound *Canadian* (however, only in the middle of the night).

THE WASAUKSING SWING BRIDGE

Better known locally as the Rose Point Swing Bridge, this structure, although small in scale, offers more interest and history than the high-level Canadian Pacific Railway (CPR) trestle.

The builder of the railway was Canada's wealthiest and most prominent railway builder of his day, John R. Booth. When he opened his massive sawmills in Ottawa and acquired extensive timber limits in Algonquin Park, he set out to cross the middle of Ontario with a rail line. Between the park and Georgian Bay he picked an unused railway charter known as the Parry Sound Colonization Railway. Although that charter stipulated that the line's terminus must be in Parry Sound, Booth opted for the less expensive and undeveloped land around Depot Harbour, where he laid out a large townsite.

But Depot Harbour was situated on Parry Island, and Booth needed to bridge a short gap between it and the mainland. To accommodate the shipping that used the channel, Booth built a swing bridge. In 1912, the Grand Trunk Railway, the line's then-owner, replaced the 1888 structure with that which still stands today.

Although the tracks are gone (as is the town of Depot Harbour), the bridge, now paved, still swings open to allow boats to pass through.

The Wasauksing railway swing bridge linking Parry Island with the mainland opens to allow the popular cruise boat, the Island Queen, *to pass.*

MANITOULIN'S SWING BRIDGE

At 172 metres long, with a swing span alone of 112 metres, the former railway bridge to the world's largest freshwater island is Ontario's longest swing bridge. The structure was completed in 1913 by the Algoma Eastern Railway, later part of the Canadian Pacific Railway (CPR). Although the original rail line was intended to continue across the island to South Baymouth, the tracks ended instead in Little Current, the busy port on Lake Huron's North Channel.

Until 1946, the bridge was kept open continuously to allow boat traffic, which included the CPR's own steamships, closing only when a train needed to cross. In that year, as automobile traffic began to replace rail travel, the Ontario Ministry of Transportation and the CPR agreed to plank in the bridge and keep it closed to allow cars to cross, opening it for the first fifteen minutes of each hour during shipping season to allow boats through — a practice it maintains to this day. After the CPR abandoned the bridge in the 1980s, the Ontario government assumed the structure. Today no rail tracks at all exist south of Espanola.

What today is formally known as the Little Current Swing Bridge is now a provincial heritage site and the island's trademark image.

THE BRIDGES OF ALGOMA COUNTRY

Algoma is noted for world famous paintings by the Group of Seven and more so for its scenic Agawa Canyon Tour Train. Two of the most impressive bridges along that line are the Bellevue Bridge and the Montreal River Bridge.

The railway was the dream of railway builder Frances Clergue. Arriving in Canada from the U.S. in 1892, he set out to build an industrial empire in Sault Ste. Marie and Sudbury. The discovery of iron ore in the hills around Wawa led him to start construction of a railway between the deposits and the Soo. But in 1903 his fortunes failed and the construction of the line did not begin again until 1909, reaching its terminus at Hearst in 1914.

The massive Bellevue Valley trestle, at the railway's mile 20, stretches 247 metres across the valley of the Goulais River, rising 31 metres where Highway 556 passes far beneath. The bridge is a plate girder resting on a series of high steel piers. The Montreal River Bridge, 472 metres long, crosses the canyon of the Montreal River atop a sturdy power dam and a dizzying 91 metres above the river. Its plate girder on steel piers curves across the valley, offering extensive views along the valley down to Lake Superior.

But perhaps the most unusual bridge of all is the "floating" bridge that crosses Oba Lake near the ghost town of Oba. Because of the soft conditions of the lake's bottom, the pilings are driven deep into the muskeg on the bottom of the lake and can be maintained only during the winter when the lake is frozen.

THE SUPERIOR BRIDGES

The Canadian Pacific Railway's west coast route hugged the mountainous shore of Lake Superior, the soaring cliffs requiring challenging bridges and tunnels. Of the many bridges and trestles along the CPR line, those over the Nipigon and Pic rivers stand out as the line's grandest.

The former is the shorter of the two, crossing above the river near the town of Nipigon, while the later tracks of the Canadian Northern Railway (CNo) were laid beneath it. It is a steel girder span on steel bents. But that at the Little Pic River is by far the more impressive. Here it leaps from a high cliff on the eastern side of the canyon and curves across the deep valley of the Little Pic River on a series of concrete, steel, and stone piers to the western cliff face, high above the waters of the lake. This engineering marvel stretches nearly half a kilometre wide and towers more than 40 metres high. Good vantage points include a lookout on the east side of the bridge beside the Trans Canada Highway, while in the valley bottom a wagon trail leads to the base of the bridge. With the CPR's frequent main line service, the lookout is one of the north's more popular train-watching spots.

Although the CNo built its route further inland, it did erect a number of important bridges. In terms of grandeur, the Pass Lake trestle rivals the CPR bridges. Now abandoned by the Canadian National Railway, it stretches for nearly a half kilometre high above the Pass Lake Road, and is one of Ontario's highest and longest rail bridges.

THUNDER BAY

This sprawling city began first as a port named Prince Arthur's Landing at the western end of Lake Superior. A short distance west, the site of the groundbreaking of the CPR's western line developed into a major rail terminus called Westfort William. As shipping grew, Port Arthur and Fort William evolved into major rail hubs. From the main rail lines, dozens of spur lines were extended to the rows of grain elevators that loomed high above the harbour. Because of the many channels carved out by the Kaministiquia River, bridges were required. This legacy has lingered in some of Ontario's more unusual railway bridges.

Two large bascule bridges carry the tracks of the CPR onto McKeller Island. Both were constructed to carry cars as well. That situated near the CPR's Fort William station carried trains on the lower deck, while automobiles plied the upper deck. Although the vehicular deck was removed in 2002, the trains still cross the lower level.

A second bascule bridge still carries cars and trains side by side on the east side of the island.

Both bridges were constructed between 1910 and 1913 by contractor A.C. Stewart. A rustic swing bridge that carries James Street traffic over the Kaministiquia River, constructed in 1912 at the west end of the city, carries rail traffic up the middle and car traffic on two outer decks. Original steel plate decking rattles beneath the car tires as they cross.

THE NORTHEAST

When the Temiskaming and Northern Ontario Railway (T&NO) was under construction from North Bay to Cochrane in 1904, some deep valleys and raging rivers got in the way, and a series of mighty bridges were needed to cross them. Most of the T&NO bridges began as wooden bridges, but were soon filled in or replaced with steel structures. A large through truss bridge today carries the tracks over the swift waters of the Montreal River at Latchford, while higher trestle bridges cross the deep valleys of the Englehart and Blanche Rivers further north. Although this latter bridge is not visible from any public road, it did offer grand vistas from the coaches of the cancelled *Northlander* passenger train. The Englehart Bridge is visible from Highway 11 at the southern entrance to Englehart.

In the 1920s, when the T&NO was extended to Moosonee in a failed attempt to establish an ocean port, its bridge builders erected a low but long bridge over the Moose River. The challenges of a rushing ice-filled river during the spring meant that piers needed to be angled upstream in order to break the onslaught of the spring ice breakup. The bridge extends more than a kilometre in two portions across the river. Further north the train rumbles across an "upside-down" bridge over the Kwataboahegan River. Due to the spring break-up on the river ice, girders which would normally be built under the bridge lie above it. This bridge lies at mileage 174. Similar structures are at mileage 176 and 180.[7]

ONTARIO'S INTERNATIONAL RAILWAY BRIDGES

Ontario can boast of having six bridges that carry rail traffic between Ontario and three neighbouring American states. Crossing between Ontario and Minnesota are those between Fort Frances and International Falls, and between Rainy River and Baudette, Minnesota. A long and multi-faceted bridge links Sault Ste. Marie, Ontario, to Sault Ste. Marie, Michigan, while three bridges span the mighty Niagara River between Ontario and New York State. A former bridge where the only piers remain visible, the Roosevelt International Bridge crossed the St. Lawrence at Cornwall, while another was never completed from Amherstburg across the Detroit River. A pair of railway tunnels completes the international links — one from Windsor to Detroit and the other from Sarnia to Port Huron.

FORT ERIE

This still-functioning bridge is known as the International Bridge and was opened in 1873. While the idea was first floated in 1856, delays, both political and technical, put off construction until after the American Civil War. Even then, technical challenges included the depth and swift flow of the river, as well as the spring build up of ice at the outlet of Lake Erie.

The bridge, while not high above the water, stretches nearly 1,000 metres and is divided into two sections, one between Fort Erie, Ontario, and Squaw Island and the other between Squaw Island and Black Rock Harbor, New York. Each section contained a swing bridge to allow boat traffic, although today only the Black Harbor portion still swings open.

The eight through trusses and swing spans rest on stone piers pointed upstream to force the break-up of floating ice.

NIAGARA FALLS

Here, over the foaming gorge, two mighty railway bridges link the two cities of Niagara Falls. The two structures almost merge at the U.S. side.

The Whirlpool Rapids Bridge, the more southerly of the two, was built by the Michigan Central Railway in 1925 and replaced the earlier cantilever bridge. Its unusual design is a steel arch bridge spanning 280 metres (860 feet) long. The bridge and railway were both acquired by the CPR, which discontinued operations in 2001 in favour of routing its trains over the International Bridge at Fort Erie. Since that time the mighty structure has sat unused and is now under threat of demolition.

The more northerly of the two bridges, now used by CN Rail, replaced an earlier suspension bridge. The first structure here was started by the Great Western Railway in 1852 and opened in 1855. With the weight of heavier and longer trains increasing, however, the first suspension bridge was soon inadequate, and in 1886 a newer and stronger suspension bridge opened. When the railway companies felt that even this would not prove sturdy enough in the long-term, they opted for a steel arch bridge instead. Construction took place within the earlier bridge and incredibly there was no disruption to train service. It was completed in 1897 and still carries CN freight and Amtrak passenger trains today. A lower deck carries commuters and bargain shoppers between the two cities.

SAULT STE. MARIE'S INTERNATIONAL RAILROAD BRIDGE

The railway bridge that crosses the St. Mary's River to link Sault Ste. Marie, Ontario, and Sault Ste. Marie, Michigan, incorporates multiple bridge styles into one design, including a vertical lift span, a bascule span, a swing span, nine camel back spans, and plate girder spans.

The bridge was built in 1887 and had to allow large lake freighters to pass through the American and Canadian locks. The main portion of the structure consists of nine camelback spans, and is anchored in the two countries. The moveable portions accommodate the boat traffic within the American and Canadian portions on each end of the camelback spans. The bascule and vertical lift spans rest over the American canal, while the swing span crosses the older and more historic Canadian lock.

Here, in an historic canal-side park, the visitor may see the Canadian end of the railway bridge. Sadly, for "security" reasons, it is not possible to view the American portion of the railway bridge except from a distance. The rail line, now part of the Canadian Pacific Railway, continues in use.[8]

TUNNELS

CANADA'S FIRST RAILWAY TUNNEL

Canada's railways often needed to blast through rocky impediments created by mountains and mesas to secure a convenient route. The Rockies and Superior's north shore offer the most dramatic examples of such engineering feats. But it was a relatively short tunnel in Brockville that took the stage as Canada's first railway tunnel.

Prior to the 1855 arrival of the Grand Trunk Railway (GT), the Brockville and Ottawa Railway had been completed to Ottawa the year before, primarily to haul lumber to the St. Lawrence for shipment to the American markets across the river. However, a large limestone outcrop stood stubbornly in the way. The town and the railway chose to avoid a costly circumvention of the rock and instead blast through it.

Canada's oldest railway tunnel is now a tourist attraction on Brockville's waterfront.

Drilling began in 1854 and six years later the first train puffed through, making it the country's first railway tunnel (even though Canada had yet to become a country). In 1863, Brockville built a city hall atop the south entrance to the tunnel, with two of its chimneys acting as vents for the tunnel.

Typically the railway builders of the time spared little expense in ensuring the stonework around the north and south entrances represented the finest in contemporary architecture. In the 1970s the Canadian Pacific Railway (which had acquired the Brockville and Ottawa line) closed the short branch through the tunnel and the portals were shut — silent, save for partying teenagers.

With the city's waterfront revitalization, Brockville expended nearly a half million dollars to refurbish the stonework on the portal, adding rail, brick walkways, and a display caboose. A historical plaque outlines the history of this early engineering feat. The north entrance, however, remains overgrown and secured behind a chain link fence.

Hamilton's Hunter Street Rail Tunnel

Although it is not a tourist attraction, the Toronto, Hamilton and Buffalo (TH&B) tunnel in Hamilton nonetheless represents Ontario's early tunnel architecture. With its stonework entrances, the Hunter Street tunnel was built by the TH&B in 1895 and runs beneath Hunter Street between Park and Queen. While the western entrance is obscured by homes, the entrance near Park Street, now built with

concrete, can be viewed from the road. The tracks continue in use by Canadian Pacific Railway freights and GO Transit commuter trains.

The Blue Tunnel

Known as the "Blue Tunnel," this stone tunnel stretches 220 metres (665 feet) beneath the Welland Canal and is said to be haunted. Some paranormal researchers have reported cases of blue mist and children's voices near the tunnel, hence its nickname. Most attribute the phenomena to a fatal train accident that occurred in 1903 and resulted in the death of two crew members.

The tunnel was part of the construction of the third version of the Welland Canal, which began in 1870. In order to move its trains more efficiently, the Great Western Railway (GW) insisted on a tunnel beneath the canal. By the time the work was done seventeen years later, the Grand Trunk (GT) had assumed operation of the railway. When the GT began upgrading and double-tracking its lines, the tunnel proved inadequate and was replaced by swing bridges, which survive today. The last train puffed through the tunnel in 1915. The winged stone entrances to the tunnel are visible beside Seaway Haulage Road to the south of Glendale Road.

The Sarnia Tunnel

Until 1891, Grand Trunk (GT) rail traffic crossed the St. Clair River by barge. That all changed in 1889 when architect Joseph Hobson, who had designed many of Ontario's grand stations, planned the world's first underwater railway tunnel. Completed in 1891, it stretched more than 1,800 metres beneath the river. In the same year, the GT added the Sarnia Tunnel station. The entrance to the original tunnel displayed the winged stone architecture found on other such tunnels. That all changed in the 1990s when the increasing use of container trains meant enlarging the tunnel. Today the fenced-off entrance offers a more ordinary concrete facade.

While most of Ontario's tracks are gone, its surviving railway bridges and tunnels still recount an almost forgotten legacy of that era.

— 3 —

BUILDING THE STATIONS

THE FIRST STATIONS

Railway stations were, and in some cases still are, the most visible and cherished features of Ontario's railway heritage. They were the centre of nearly every small town and were where the townspeople most directly interacted with the railways. It was where they greeted long-lost relatives, where they bade farewell to loved ones, and where they embarked upon an adventure themselves.

Ontario's railways have been building stations since 1853, and continue to do so. VIA Rail opened its latest station in Belleville in 2012. Over time, styles have ranged wildly from the simplest board and batten buildings in the beginning to more elaborate structures with friezes, gargoyles, arches,

pillars, and high towers that served no purpose at all, during the heyday of rail travel. Today, VIA's newest buildings in Belleville and London reflect the latest in modern architecture.

Ontario's first stations were those erected in 1853 by the Ontario, Simcoe, and Huron Railway, which in 1853 sent the first steam trains puffing from Toronto's waterfront to Machell's Corners (today's Aurora.) The sole surviving example of the line's first-generation stations stands in the King Township Heritage Village and features a simple style with arched windows and a roofline that extends over the platform.

From 1854–55 the Great Western Railway (GW) was quickly laying its tracks from Niagara Falls to Windsor, while simultaneously throwing together a line of simple stations. Nearly all its first-generation stations were identical with a wide, low roof and board and batten siding. The only surviving example stands near the tracks in Grimsby and now serves as an antique store

The Grand Trunk (GT), which in 1856 was hard on the heels of the Great Western, paid more attention to their first stations, spurning the GW's cheap "American" style and copying a solid stone design used at Kenilworth, England. As with those of the GW, the GT-built stations that were low and wide. But instead of wood, they chose stone and brick, and embellished the style with arched French doors around the structure.

Slightly different versions appeared in Belleville and Kingston with a second-floor mansard roof.

As the rail network boomed into a spider's web of lines across Ontario, each successive railway line created its own distinctive station style. First generation stations were often very simple in design. Railway lines that endured beyond those formative years including the GW, the GT, and the Canadian Pacific Railway replaced most of their first-generation stations to serve growing demand and changing tastes.

THE CANADIAN PACIFIC RAILWAY

After the Canadian Pacific Railway (CPR) broke ground for its new national line in the 1870s, it continued to add trackage in Ontario even as late as 1912, and introduced a variety of station patterns over that time.

Among the CPR's earliest were those erected in the 1870s on the Toronto, Grey and Bruce and the Credit Valley railways. Although many were little more than boxes, the railway did add a few that sported a decorative corner turret. While none remain in active service, examples of these were relocated and survive in Streetsville, Milton, and Smithville. Toronto's Don Station, built by the CPR at Queen Street, now resides in Roundhouse Park. Interestingly, the Hamilton and Northwestern Railway structure copied that style for its Craigleith station.

The Ontario and Quebec Railway, a line built between Agincourt and Perth through the 1880s, adopted an early plan, nicknamed the "Van Horne" style. One of the company's simplest, it was initiated by president William Cornelius Van Horne in the 1880s. This simple plan — wooden, two storeys, with gable ends — could be sent across the country to local contractors who could have the building up sometimes in days. Most were later replaced as part of CPR's upgrading and regrettably no such CPR stations have survived anywhere in Canada. Those on the Ottawa and Quebec (O&Q), however, survived until the end of rail service. Now all are gone. The last in Tweed was used as a lumber office.

The CPR's 1908 main line from Bolton to Sudbury relied almost solely on a pair of Western plan stations, which included a two-storey hip-gable roof and a hip-gable dormer on the second floor. The other displayed a steep storey-and-a-half bell-cast roof with a dormer for the agent's quarters. Nearly all are gone now, torn down during the late 1970s and early 1980s within a few years of each other. The best example of the former is that relocated from Nashville to Islington Avenue in Kleinburg, moved at the urging of Kleinburg resident and author, Pierre Berton, whose The National Dream series celebrated Canada's railway heritage in print.

An example of the latter style was that relocated from Alliston to the grounds of a railway enthusiast in Tottenham and repainted to its original maroon and yellow colour scheme. It is now his home.

Although rarely used, the CPR also inaugurated the "witch's hat" station, where the circular waiting room incorporated a conical roof said to resemble a witch's hat. Surviving examples include those at Goderich, Parry Sound, and Orangeville (relocated). The Grand Trunk adopted this style with stations in Blyth and Uxbridge.

But the CPR did not shy away from coming up with some of Ontario's finer architect-designed station buildings. Perhaps its most striking station accomplishment was its 1916 North Toronto station. It still stands, carefully restored, serving as home for a liquor store.

After the Second World War, the CPR introduced yet another more modern style. Known as the "international" style, the buildings were flat-roofed and incorporated many of the art deco features of the pre-war period. These included flat, rounded eaves and stand-alone station names. While most of these appeared in the post-war pulp mill towns of northern Ontario, a few were added in the south. The only survivor, either north or south, is that in Owen Sound, built in 1948 to replace the original Toronto, Grey and Bruce station. Tracks were lifted in the 1990s, and by 2012 the station remained vacant.

WOODSTOCK AND GALT

No doubt the CPR built a number of divisional stations to the style found in the two southwestern Ontario communities of Woodstock and Galt, but they are the only to survive in Ontario. Both were designed by Edward Maxwell, one of that railway's busiest architects. Both feature a Tudor-style half-timber gable above the entrances and both are brick on a limestone base. Stone quoins mark the buildings' corners and arched transoms the main doorways. Both stations remain in railway use today. The station in Galt also retains its similarly styled freight shed. While the yards in Galt are silent now, those in Woodstock remain filled with railway rolling stock.

HAMILTON'S TH&B STATION

In 1895, the Toronto, Hamilton and Buffalo Railway (TH&B), an American line, entered Ontario with its plan to link the Canada Southern Railway and Michigan Central lines with the busy harbours in Hamilton where they erected a large Italianate stone station.

But as the 1930s arrived with increased road traffic, pressure was exerted on the TH&B to join the Canadian National Railway (CNR) in a union station. Instead the railway opted to simply elevate its tracks and build a new station of its own. To do so, the railway hired architects Fellheimer and Wagner who brought to Hamilton their art deco flair with the use of stepped lines, wraparound windows, and interior use of steel railings. It was unlike any station Ontario had ever seen.

After the Canadian Pacific Railway (CPR) acquired the TH&B in 1988, it ended passenger service, downsized its workforce, and allowed the building to deteriorate. In 1995, after passenger service ended at the CN station, the City of Hamilton and GO Transit took over the building, repairing it and converting it to a GO Transit station and interurban bus depot. Once more, the interior art deco features such as railings and chandeliers made the building distinctive from the beginning. The second floor mezzanine also contains historic photos and railway equipment, such as an early dispatcher's board.

THE GREAT WESTERN GROUP

Over the nearly three decades during which the Great Western Railway operated in Ontario before its amalgamation with the Grand Trunk in 1882, architect Joseph Hobson created a string of more elaborate stations to replace those first-generation buildings.

CHATHAM

Hobson designed this elegant building in 1882 with three prominent gables, two hip-roofed cross-gables at the ends, and a peaked gable in the centre. The building, constructed of brick and now painted red, features gothic-style pointed windows. Freight and express functions were under the end gables, the operator's office under the centre gable, while separate men's and women's waiting rooms were in between. Originally the structure also contained a lunch room and boasted a slate roof. It continues to serve VIA Rail.

WOODSTOCK

Hobson's Great Western station in Woodstock has the air of an English country station. This two-storey Gothic revival structure, built in 1882, features a remarkable variety of gable styles, no two alike. A large hip-gable dominates the front while a series of peak gables surround the second floor. Brick pilasters and arches are featured on the doors and above the windows. The southeast corner of the ground floor and second floor were designed for the station master and his family but the second floor is empty now. While the freight section was removed in recent years, VIA Rail restored the building in 1992. The station still has an agent to serve VIA Rail customers daily.

A Toronto-bound VIA Rail train pulls into the elegant Chatham station, designed by Joseph Hobson.

NIAGARA FALLS

At this customs entry point and divisional yard, Hobson designed a much larger station at Niagara Falls (then called Clifton). Styled in the Gothic revival era, the centre portion of this large brick building extends two floors where various staff were once situated. A customs shed and freight shed extend the building well to the west. Hobson's trademark hip-gables dominate the ends of both the lower and upper stories, while a peak gable extends above the bay window. It was completed in 1879 when the earlier wooden station burned. Now modernized, the station continues to serve VIA and Amtrak customers while Ontario's GO Transit has extended service to the site as well. The Great Western erected stations similar to it in Niagara Falls, Hamilton, London, and Windsor, but all were subsequently replaced.

Sarnia

When the Grand Trunk absorbed the Great Western, Joseph Hobson came along with it as architect. As a result, he created another of his works of art in Sarnia. The station was built in 1891 well southeast of the city to accommodate the traffic through the newly opened Sarnia to Port Huron tunnel. Built of brick, the station features a prominent oversized hip-gable above the centre portion and lower hip cross-gables above the two ends. In 2012, due to cutbacks imposed by the Harper government, VIA Rail was forced to reduce service to Sarnia, despite local demand.

Ingersoll

Although the Great Western (GW) had amalgamated with the Grand Trunk (GT) by the time the former GW architect Joseph Hobson designed this station in 1889, it bears few of his earlier Gothic revival characteristics, with the exception of its pointed windows. Reflecting a period of cost-cutting by the GT, it is a simple massing with a steep roof and a single gable over the operators' bay. Unfortunately, the original yellow and red brickwork was painted over. Although federally designated, the station sits vacant and vandalized.

THE GRAND TRUNK'S LEGACY

Kingston

Kingston's historic "outer" station has not enjoyed a happy existence. With the opening of a new suburban station in 1974, a steep curve on the tracks to the old station was bypassed and the station closed. Following a few fleeting re-uses, it has sat derelict, subject to demolition by neglect. A fire in 1996 ravaged the interior causing the wonderful mansard roof to collapse.

Built in 1855, this first-generation Grand Trunk (GT) station was one of only two that incorporated a second floor (the other being Belleville), which was added in the 1870s. Arched windows line the front and rear, while a freight door lies at the end. A second brick station was built to the east in 1898. A few original limestone railway workers' homes still stand on the east side of Montreal Road. According to *historicplaces.ca* it is the only remaining GT headquarters building to survive on the old main line.

St. Mary's

It is fortunate indeed that one of southwestern Ontario's most attractive towns would retain a pair of attractive heritage stations. The older of the two is an original first-generation Grand Trunk (GT) station north of the current town at a location known as St. Mary's Junction. Built in 1856 on the GT's Toronto to Sarnia route, it became a "junction" when the GT built a connecting line to its newly acquired Great Western line in London. The exterior retains the original French doors, which unlike other similar first-generation stations, were not altered to become windows. Currently it is undergoing restoration.

Of the thirty-eight such first-generation "Kenilworth" stations, seven remain. Port Hope still survives as Canada's oldest station in continuous use. The Napanee station, while still a VIA stop, now houses an operation known as Workshop Wizard. Prescott and Ernestown survive: the former houses a museum while the latter sits abandoned. The former Brighton station is the focus of a railway museum and yard display known as Memory Junction. The original Grand Trunk station in Georgetown was renovated in 1904 to include a raised roof and a tower on one corner.

The second of St. Mary's two heritage stations was built by the GT in 1912 nearer the centre of the town. Today it houses a VIA Rail waiting room and tourist office. Architecturally it features a sweeping bell-cast roof with a semi-conical gable above the bay. A rounded bay window and corners add to the allure of the building.

THE GRAND TRUNK'S HEYDAY

After the Grand Trunk (GT) had absorbed the Great Western (GW), the Midland, and a number of smaller lines, the economy boomed and the GT embarked upon a major upgrade of its system. Tracks were doubled, bridges filled, and stations replaced. Between 1891 and 1911, the GT erected new stations at Stratford, Brampton, Brantford, Berlin (now Kitchener), Grimsby, St. Mary's, and Guelph. All except that in Grimsby, which burned, survive and remain in railway use.

The big trend of the period was towers. Useless though they were, station towers had become an urban status symbol. The more prominent of Ontario's towered stations were in Stratford, Kitchener, Guelph, and Brantford.

BRANTFORD

Brantford was a decidedly late comer to the Grand Trunk system. Although it had been a stop on the Buffalo, Brantford and Goderich line, the GT had initially bypassed the town in favour of a more direct line between Lynden and Paris to the north. But when the railway began its upgrading, the GT rerouted its line through Brantford and abandoned the original section.

The Grand Trunk (GT) erected in Brantford one of its most elaborate stations in southwestern Ontario. The tower extends a full four storeys, and rises above a high, rounded waiting room which features a conical roof, brass chandelier, and tiled wainscotting. The rounded operator's bay window boasts an octagonal roof, while the entire roof is covered in red tiles, as is a covered porte cochère that marks the street entrance. The architects were the Detroit firm of Spier and Rohns, which also designed the GT's magnificent stations throughout Michigan. Now owned by VIA Rail, the Brantford station remains one of the busiest VIA stations in southwestern Ontario.

The Coffee Stop Café occupies the former freight shed and is connected to the main station by a canopied walkway.

GUELPH

The Grand Trunk added its line through Guelph in 1858 and built a standard first-generation "Kenilworth"-style station. However, within twenty years Guelph had boomed to a population of 8,500 and the city leaders began to lobby for a larger and more fitting station, insisting upon a tower as well.

Opened in 1911, the solid station was constructed of brick on granite with a high tower above

The Brantford VIA station reflects a period when the Grand Trunk was featuring towers on its stations.

the porte cochère entrance. In 2012, GO Transit added a few shelters to the east of the station.

KITCHENER

Like most other communities along the Grand Trunk (GT) line, Berlin's first GT station was the typical "Kenilworth" type. But by 1896 the city's growth required a larger structure and the GT assigned architect Hobson to the job. He designed a brick building with a Gothic tower, sporting a steeply pitched roof. A large gable marked the street entrance while small dormers punctuated the trackside roofline. Berlin became Kitchener during the First World War. In 1966, the CNR, then the owners, removed all the rooftop embellishments in order to modernize the building. It continues to serve VIA passengers today, although requirements for a new combined GO and VIA facility appear to have doomed this historic structure to demolition.

STRATFORD

This town, now widely known for its annual Shakespeare Festival, has a much longer and deeper railway history. Originally it was the junction of the Grand Trunk (GT) and Buffalo and Lake Huron Railway, and so the station took the name "Stratford Junction." However, in 1911, with competition looming from the Canadian Pacific Railway and the Canadian Northern Railway (neither of which showed up), the GT enlarged the facilities creating a major divisional point. A new two-storey brick station on a St. Mary's limestone base contained offices on the second floor and a 20-metre high castellated tower. While most of the earlier railway buildings have long gone, as has the tower, the station remains a prominent landmark.

BRAMPTON

Brampton's new replacement station came with towers as well, in fact, three of them. When the Grand Trunk (GT) built its first standard "Kenilworth" station, the village was still little more than a stopping place on the Hurontario Street settlement road. But when new industries arrived, especially brickmaking, and the town became a county seat, the GT replaced the original station with a more castle-like structure. With three towers on the street-side entrance and a two-storey gable above the operator's bay, the new station combined the rounded arches of the Richardsonian style with the towers of the Château style.

While it remains close to the city's downtown, it is sadly lost amid a sea of cars belonging to the hoards of commuters who daily climb aboard the Toronto-bound GO trains.

COBOURG

Unlike the stations along the Grand Trunk Railway's western line, those along its eastern line between Toronto and Quebec largely remained unchanged. The largest second-generation GT station to be built on this section and to remain in use is that in Cobourg. When American iron manufacturers began to arrive in Cobourg in the late 1800s and build their grand summer homes, the GT decided to replace its original wooden station in 1911 with a brick-on-stone Richardsonian Romanesque building that measured 10 metres by 50 metres. The station continues to be among the line's busiest and in 1994 VIA Rail undid some of the unsympathetic CNR alterations, restoring the wainscotting and the original ceiling.

In 2012 the waiting room was extended into the former baggage area, while access to the north tracks was improved as well.

Gananoque Junction

In 1856, when the builders of the Grand Trunk (GT) bypassed the St. Lawrence River port of Gananoque, the town business owners began to lobby furiously for a link. The GT had originally placed one of their standard "Kenilworth" stations on the line where a small community called Cheeseborough grew up, but a long arduous road journey was still needed to reach Gananoque.

In 1889, an 8 kilometre railway, known as the Thousand Islands Railway (TIR), was built from the Grand Trunk (GT) to the river. When the GT awoke to the growing popularity of the new line with tourists heading for the Thousand Islands, it eventually bought the TIR and built a newer and more decorative station at a new junction. Although diminutive, it sports a small central tower

and a stepped bell-cast roofline. CN Rail shut down passenger service on the TIR in 1962 and abandoned the line entirely in 1995, lifting the tracks as well. This rural station still receives two VIA Rail trains a day. A small TIR station shelter still stands in downtown Gananoque on the main street

Brockville

By 1856, Brockville, on the shores of the St. Lawrence River in eastern Ontario, had already become a busy railway junction with the Brockville and Ottawa Railway, and the Grand Trunk established a divisional point here. The station style was an extended version of its Kenilworth stations to accommodate the additional divisional functions. Although the divisional functions and structures have vanished, the station sees several trains a day, both passenger and freight.

THE GT EXPANDS

Although more than 115 railway charters were approved in Ontario, few were ever built. Most were resource lines to haul lumber or minerals from Ontario's hinterlands to its ports or industries. Eventually, the Grand Trunk (GT) added several of these to its growing network. Stations on the resource lines were simple, wooden single-storey structures with little need for architectural embellishment. Occasionally the GT replaced or upgraded these simple buildings, although the replacements remained modest in size. Most of these branches have been abandoned and their stations, the few that have survived, gained new uses, many as homes, businesses, or museums.

MARKHAM AND UNIONVILLE

Of the few remaining resource stations that still see trains, those that do include Markham and Unionville. Both were located on the 1873 Toronto and Nipissing Railway which the Grand Trunk took over in 1881. Unlike stations on other lines, those in Markham and Unionville are first-generation Toronto and Nipissing Railway buildings. Both are low and wide with a roofline that extends over the platform, although that in Markham is considerably larger. After years of neglect by the Canadian National Railway, both have been restored, that in Unionville to become a community facility and that in Markham as a GO station and event venue.

MAPLE, AURORA, AND NEWMARKET

Another line absorbed by the Grand Trunk (GT) was the Ontario, Simcoe, and Huron Railway (OS&H), built to connect Toronto with Allandale on Lake Simcoe, which marked the starting point for the Northern and Northwestern Railway to North Bay. The original OS&H stations were the usual simple board-and-batten stations, the last of which now rests on the grounds of the King Museum Village on King Road. The GT replaced

the other originals with what is known as their "stick-style" station.

These attractive board-and-batten buildings featured extra fret work in the front and end gable and finials on the roofline. While most were removed by the CNR, survivors include the refurbished GO stations in Aurora and Maple, and the Chamber of Commerce in Newmarket. Although less embellished than the others, the former GT station in Bradford has similarly been restored and it too has become a GO station.

The Grand Trunk featured fanciful fretwork on several of its stations, such as that in Maple which now serves GO Transit commuters.

ALEXANDRIA

In 1904 the Grand Trunk (GT) took over the Canada Atlantic Railway (CAR) and in 1917 replaced Alexandria's original structure with a more stylish brick station. While not large, the unusual bracketed overhanging hip-gable above the bay window accentuates its size. Still serving VIA's Montreal to Ottawa trains, the interior offers a number of historic photos including those of Charles M. Hays, ill-fated president of the GT who went down with the *Titanic*, and J.R. Booth, builder of the CAR.

Another active station on the Montreal-Ottawa line is that at Casselman. Its plain single-storey style is more similar to the simple pattern book-station plans used by the CNR.

ST. CATHARINES

In 1916, the Grand Trunk replaced St. Catharines' Great Western station with a simple low-rise brick structure with a semi-circular capped parapet wall above the entrance, flanked by pilasters topped with balls and pedestrals. Still in use by VIA and GO, it fittingly lies on Great Western Avenue.

UXBRIDGE

In 1871, the Toronto and Nipissing (T&N) Railway extended its route from Uxbridge to Coboconk. It was chartered by the Gooderham and Worts Distillery in Toronto to ship raw material to its factories. The T&N established its main yard at Uxbridge where it erected a low, wooden station, similar to those still standing in Markham and Unionville. In 1904, the Grand Trunk (GT) replaced the old station with a rare, decorative new "witch's hat" style that displays a rounded waiting room with a cone-shaped roof.

After Canadian National acquired the GT and lifted the rails between Uxbridge and Coboconk, the station became a residence. Then, with the inauguration of the popular York and Durham Heritage Railway in 1995, the station was restored and became a boarding point for the historic trains. Today it is a designated heritage building.

PORT STANLEY

Shortly after the Great Western arrived in London, the railway realized the value of a link with Lake Erie's port, and in 1856 the London and Port Stanley Railway did just that. The current station, which is the ticketing office for the Port Stanley Terminal Railway tourist train, was built in 1908 by the Grand Trunk and replaced a simpler wooden structure. This single-storey stuccoed station features few embellishments other than a gable above the operator's bay. The station also contains a gift shop.

UNION

North America's smallest "Union" station, this preserved stuccoed shelter is named for a nearby village, not for any role in serving multiple railways. Despite its diminutive size, its architectural flair includes rounded windows among other decorative features. This Union station is a stop on the Port Stanley Terminal Railway.

AFTER THE GRAND TRUNK

The years of the First World War were not kind to Canada's heavily subsidized railways. Funds went instead towards the war, and sent lines like the Grand Trunk and Canadian Northern into bankruptcy. To save the railways, the federal government legislated into existence a new government railway, the Canadian National Railway (CNR). As this was still the heyday of rail travel, the CNR too embarked on some station-building of its own. While most of its small-town stations were simple and pragmatic in design, it put its key architect to work to design its new urban terminals, and that architect was John Schofield.

HAMILTON'S CN STATION.

One of Schofield's grand achievements was the new Canadian National station in Hamilton. The city's original Great Western Railway station had been a typical low, wide wooden structure on Stuart Street. In 1875, Joseph Hobson designed a replacement station of two storeys and his trademark Gothic Revival hip-gable roofline. That lasted until the 1930s when Schofield, as part of Hamilton's "city beautiful" movement, created a neo-classical structure which featured four two-storey pillars interspersed with friezes of railway scenes and a grand lobby marked with brass chandeliers and blue-and-gold ornamentation. A wide lawn in front allowed an unfettered view of the grand new building.

It opened in 1931, but closed in 1990 and began to deteriorate.

Then along came a most unusual saviour, Hollywood. Taking over the station to film *The Long Kiss Goodnight*, the movie-makers spent $1 million in repairs. Soon after, the benevolent Labourers International Union of North American acquired the building and completed the renovations, converting it to offices and an event venue. Landscaping and statuary now decorate the wide lawn in front and the building goes by the name "LIUNA Station." Discussions began in 2012 to propose restoring its railway use.

Hamilton's CNR station was built as part of a city beautiful movement. It is now known as the LIUNA station.

CORNWALL

East of Brockville, along the shores of the St. Lawrence River, the Grand Trunk had erected a string of its standard stations. Then in 1956, the rising waters of the St. Lawrence Seaway forced the removal of the stations and indeed the very towns that they served. In their place, the CNR built a string of five modernistic stations with flat roofs, bright, spacious waiting rooms, and wide windows. The largest of the group, that at Cornwall, remains a passenger station for travellers on VIA Rail. That at Morrisburg remains in CN Rail use, while the others have predictably been demolished.

TORONTO'S UNION STATION

Toronto has always had "union" stations, ever since the 1850s when a variety of railways began to converge on the city's waterfront. But as rail travel boomed, each quickly became obsolete and was replaced. The devastating fire of 1904 cleared the ground for yet another new union station. In 1906, the Toronto Terminals Railway (TTR) was created to undertake the task.

But, typically, Toronto politics delayed the decision as to the type of building needed and it was not until 1914 that the TTR finally hired the firm of Ross and MacDonald along with architect John Lyle to create what would become one of North America's finest union stations. Another dozen years would pass, however, before the Prince of Wales formally opened it in 1927.

Right from the main entrance, a row of pillars stand guard and lead travellers into the Grand Hall, a high, vaulted chamber modelled after the Santa Maria Maggiore in Rome. Intricate ceiling work

and friezes marking the then-various train destinations loom high above the ticket windows and the circular information booth. In 2012, a new Panorama Lounge opened for first class travellers with retro decorative features, such as woodwork and lighting, which reflect the style of the rail's heyday of the 1920s and 1930s.

OTTAWA'S AIRPORT-LIKE UNION STATION

Throughout the 1960s, railway tracks criss-crossing downtown Ottawa were considered unsightly, and with the 1967 Centennial celebrations looming, they needed to go. The attractive 1916 Union Station on Wellington Street was closed while Parkin and Associates, who designed Toronto airport's first "Terminal One," designed for Ottawa a new suburban air-terminal-style station with a flat roof, expansive windows, and circular ticket booth in the centre.

During the 1960s the Canadian National Railway (CNR) added other modernistic suburban stations in Oshawa, Oakville, and Windsor. These have recently been altered by VIA Rail with steep, towered retro rooflines. During this period the CNR replaced the London Grand Trunk station with an office tower that contained a cramped waiting room on the ground floor. This in turn was fortunately demolished and replaced with a larger VIA station that incorporates such retro features as a tower, high steel-beamed ceiling in the waiting room, and a period clock. VIA's latest architectural addition is the ultra-modern station opened in Belleville in 2012, while at the same time saving the historic stone 1857 GT station.

VIA Rail's newest station, and one of its busiest, is the modernistic Belleville station, opened in 2012. The Grand Trunk's 1857 station is to the left.

THE LEGACY OF THE CANADIAN NORTHERN RAILWAY

Although a late-comer to the southern Ontario railway scene, the Canadian Northern Railway (CNo) brought its ubiquitous rural prairie-style stations to the province. With their trademark pyramid roofs, the stations appeared along key rail lines which linked Toronto with Ottawa and Sudbury. For larger towns and cities, the CNo lured architect Ralph Benjamin Pratt away from the Canadian Pacific Railway to create what remain today as some of this province's architectural masterpieces. None of the CNo stations remains in railway use.[1]

PORT HOPE

In 1913, the Canadian Northern's vital link from Toronto to Ottawa was finished, and here it decided to create a more elaborate style of station. For Port Hope, Belleville, and Cobourg, the Canadian Northern Railway (CNo) engaged Pratt to design a Château-style building. Two storeys in height and constructed of brick, the stations exhibited an octagonal end waiting room and two-storey gable. Of the three, only that at Port Hope survives and is now a government office. The tracks have been gone for more than half a century.

SOLINA

The rural Canadian Northern (CNo) station that served the village of Solina, near Oshawa, is a rare in situ surviving example of a standard-plan CNo prairie station. The only other examples of this style remaining in southern Ontario are those from Rockland, near Ottawa, and Southwood in Muskoka, both relocated as private homes.

SMITHS FALLS

Here too, Pratt put his skills to work to come up with another Château. Although single-storey, it boasts a prominent octagonal tower above its bay window. Constructed in the brick-on-stone style, it remains on its right-of-way and has become the focus of the Eastern Ontario Railway Museum.

AMERICAN INVADERS

Although it was called the "Canada Southern" Railway, the CASO line, built in 1873, was in truth simply an American railway shortcut across southwestern Ontario from Fort Erie to its terminus at Corunna on the St. Clair River, south of Sarnia. Most of its stations were of the very simple, wooden American style with few or no architectural embellishments. Most are now gone, or have been relocated, as are the rail lines themselves. Comber's now-CN station, although federally designated, sits vacant and deteriorating beside overgrown tracks.

ST. THOMAS

Due to the distance between Fort Erie and the St. Clair River, a divisional point was needed at the halfway mark, and that was St. Thomas. With its flat terrain and access to water, the Canada Southern Railway chose this site to erect it massive yards, roundhouse, locomotive repair shop, car shop, and what would prove to be one of Ontario's grandest station buildings.

The attractive stone station in Essex, Ontario reflects the Richardsonian Romanesque influence in station-building.

Italianate in style, with 400,000 bricks and measuring 12 metres wide by an incredible 100 metres long, the station building contained a fine dining room and separate men's and women's waiting rooms on the ground floor, and the offices of the draftsmen, solicitors, yardmasters, and quarters for the dining-room staff on the second floor. Two arched throughways connected the two sides of the station. At one point, three lines used the station, including the Canadian Pacific Railway's Credit Valley tracks on the north side. Over its lifetime, twenty-five different rail lines used the building.

After CN Rail shut down the rail operations, the yards sat empty and overgrown and the roundhouse and locomotive shop were removed, leaving only the station, car shop, and a switching tower.

ESSEX

In 1887, the CASO added one of Ontario's more delightful stone stations to the village of Essex, then an important railway junction. Influenced by renowned American station architect H.H. Richardson, the station included arched windows a rounded operators' bay, extensions, and a small tower above the street entrance. Passenger service ended prior to 1975 when a twenty-year restoration began. The station now appears as it did in 1907.[2]

NORTHERN ONTARIO'S RAILWAY HERITAGE

ON THE TRAIL OF THE NORTHLANDER

In a short-sighted effort to make its Ontario Northland Railway more salable, the Ontario Government in 2012 ended the more than century-old passenger service on the legendary *Northlander*. Still, its heritage lingers in the stations that line its historic route which links Toronto with North Bay, Cochrane, and, ultimately, Moosonee.

In 1888, the Northern and Northwestern Railway (also known as the Northern and Pacific Junction Railway) began to lay tracks from Atherley to Callander, near North Bay on Lake Nipissing, where it would meet the rails of the Canadian Pacific Railway. Along the route, it built a series of first-generation stations, most of which stood two storeys with hip-gables at each end and a centre gable above the operator's bay. It was along this route that the *Northlander* made its way to North Bay.

WASHAGO

While station and tracks are long gone from Atherley, the Washago station yet survives, today used by CN maintenance crews. The current building, however, was one erected by the Canadian Northern Railway in 1912 when it was laying its line from Toronto to Sudbury and replaced the first Northern and Northwestern Railway building. Its low roofline with extended eaves and gables over the bay and the ends was a standard Canadian

Northern style found along the southern portion of this line.

GRAVENHURST

Gravenhurst is one of the line's more attractive stations. Built by the Grand Trunk after it assumed the Northern and Northwestern, this wooden station contains an octagonal waiting room at the north end of the station where today's travellers can purchase bus tickets or enjoy a snack from the snack bar. A separate building to the south contained the freight shed, while yet a third building contained the dining room and is now a veterinary clinic. In 1983, the station was upgraded by the Ministry of Transportation as part of a program to convert rail stations to multi-modal transportation hubs.

HUNTSVILLE

This more recent station was added by the Canadian National Railway in 1937, replacing the standard NNW building. After allowing the building to deteriorate, the CN sold the station to the Town of Huntsville, which turned it into a waiting room and a museum that includes a Grand Trunk weigh scale. Constructed of brick, it has few adornments, although the extended hip-gable above the operator's bay breaks the monotony.

SOUTH RIVER

Here too the NNW established a divisional point with a coal chute, water tower, and roundhouse.

Although smaller than most divisional stations, the building in South River is the last original NNW station to survive. Wood on stone, the station has a more decorative gable above the bay window, and thanks to years of community fundraising has been restored and now houses a museum. One of the line's two surviving coal chutes survives here as well. The other is at Washago.

TO ARCTIC TIDEWATER

NORTH BAY

It is from this city that the trail of the *Northlander* owes its origins to a provincially chartered railway. In 1903, the Temiskaming and Northern Ontario Railway (T&NO), now the Ontario Northland Railway (ONR), began constructing a colonization railway from North Bay to open up the area around New Liskeard. However, the spectacular silver strike at Cobalt spurred the T&NO to extend the new line from North Bay to meet the federal government's proposed new national line, the National Transcontinental Railway (NTR) at Cochrane, where the two railways erected a large union station.

As the T&NO opened the farmlands, the forests, and the mineral deposits of northeastern Ontario, the railway placed stations at 10–12 mile intervals. The first-generation stations were a storey and a half with steep bell-cast roofs and a dormer above the operator's bay window. Others were a full two storeys, such as those which stood at Earlton and Tomiko. Within a few years the T&NO replaced a few first-generation stations with much more appealing buildings, such as those at Cobalt and Temagami. The remainder were demolished.

Until 1995, the ONR operated from the Canadian National Railway's North Bay station, built originally by the Canadian Northern Railway (CNo). In that year the ONR opened a large, bright new station facility of its own with dispatching facilities for train crews as well. A large waiting room provides facilities for bus travellers only, now that train service has ended.

TEMAGAMI

That at Temagami was constructed in 1909 of stone with a half-timbered Tudor-revival gable, an extension of the bay, and separate men's and ladies' waiting rooms. The style was designed to attract tourists to the steamers waiting behind the station to transport them to the resorts on Lake Temagami. The original first-generation station lingered for a number of years as a restaurant. Recently however, a station restoration trust led by Clare and Richard Smirden has restored the waiting room which now houses a gift shop, as well as the entire exterior. This building is one of northeastern Ontario's more spectacular buildings, and a tourist attraction in its own right.

The **Northlander** *passenger train, since discontinued, glides up to the Temagami station, one of northeastern Ontario's most attractive stations.*

The Cornwall station is a rare 1950s-style CN station, and the last of the five built due to the flooding from the St. Lawrence Seaway.

COBALT

Cobalt had by 1909 become the boom town of the northeast, with extensive silver deposits luring more than 20,000 residents. The Temiskaming and Northern Ontario (T&NO) hired architect John

Lyle to design a station befitting such a booming town. His brick station measures 50 metres by 10 metres with a vaulted waiting room that measures 22 metres by 10 metres. The station stands two storeys high with single-storey wings, and a semi-circular arched dormer above the second floor.

ENGLEHART

Early stations at Haileybury, Earlton, and New Liskeard are gone now, the latter replaced with a modern flat-roofed building. The current building at Englehart replaced the original divisional station in the mid-1990s, but is nonetheless an attractive two-storey station with a series of dormers along the roof. It continues in its role as a divisional station with an extensive yard that is usually filled with lumber trains.

MATHESON

The next station that can be called a "heritage" building is that at Matheson. The original building was destroyed during the deadly forest fires that ravaged the region in 1911 and 1914, claiming hundreds of lives. Were it not for the *Northlander* coming to the rescue, many more would have perished. With the end of rail service, the brick station now serves as a bus depot and tourist information centre. Former T&NO stations in Val Gagne and Ramore have found new uses and remodelled accordingly.

COCHRANE

This brings the line to Cochrane and what was originally an important junction with the National Transcontinental Railway. That railway was part of the dream of Prime Minister Sir Wilfrid Laurier to create a transcontinental rival to the Canadian Pacific Railway. Reaching Cochrane ahead of the National Transcontinental Railway (NTR), the Temiskaming and Northern Ontario (T&NO) once again hired John Lyle to design the grand two-storey station which housed dispatchers and other vital railway functions. The brick building boasted a cupola, cross-gables, and a string of dormers. Inside were a dining room and a vaulted waiting room. The NTR shared the space as a divisional point, while its track passed on the north side of the station.

The Canadian National Railway, which had absorbed the NTR, removed much of the roof ornamentation. More recently, the Ontario Northland Railway has added a new waiting room, while enlarging the building with the installation of second floor inn and a new restaurant adjacent to it.

TIMMINS

When the Temiskaming and Northern Ontario (T&NO) extended a branch to the goldfields of Timmins from Porquis Junction it designed a solid yellow brick station as befitting the status of this booming gold mining capital. This long single-storey structure rests typically at the head of Timmins' downtown main street. Although the tracks are gone, the waiting room and ticketing area retain many of the early architectural features. The building now serves the Ontario Northland and Timmins Transit buses. New bus bays occupy the site of the former tracks.

Moosonee

In 1932, in an effort to develop an ocean port, the T&NO extended its tracks to Arctic tidewater at a Révillon Frères trading post called Moosonee. Here it built a diminutive wooden station which yet stands at the head of the rugged main street. Although the port never developed due to shifting sand bars in the river, Moosonee has become a popular tourist destination for goose hunters, and for those travelling on the *Polar Bear Express* to visit the historic Hudson's Bay trading post site on Moose Factory Island or to stay in the new Cree-run Eco-Lodge.

THE ALGOMA CENTRAL RAILWAY

Sault Ste. Marie

Having given up on its original dream name, the Algoma Central and James Bay Railway, the ACR, was content to terminate at Hearst on the National Transcontinental Railway. While the grand and historic stations at Hearst and Oba are regrettably both gone, the ACR's heritage stations at Sault Ste. Marie, Searchmont, and Hawk Junction remain.

Now corporate offices for the ACR's current owner, CN Rail, the grand former downtown station rises three storeys and is constructed of the familiar rich red sandstone of the Soo area. Built in 1912, following the revival of the ACR's fortunes, the former station is also the focus for the Station Mall. Meanwhile, a newer station facility built to handle the tourists boarding the popular Agawa Canyon tour train stands a short distance west.

Searchmont

Although it has been designated as "protected" under federal heritage legislation, in 2012 the two-storey station at Searchmont appeared to be in a sorry state of repair. Here is another case where a community's railway station has been "protected" from railway demolition, but no one in the community has yet come forth to rescue it. The octagonal bay window extends to the upper floor which housed the accommodation for the agent and his family. An octagonal gable tops off the bay window. What was once a rounded waiting room was destroyed by fire in 1929.

Hawk Junction

At Hawk Junction, a two-storey brick station likely dates back to the destruction of the community by fire in 1929. It remains a busy boarding point for cottagers and lodge guests bound for their remote recreational retreats along the line. The waiting room still offers a ticket booth, its walls plastered with historic images and clippings. The yard contains a small number of sidings and quarters for the small CN Rail crew stationed here. When the iron mines in Wawa were still operating, a branch led from Hawk Junction to Michipicoten Harbour on Lake Superior where the remains of the ore dock and coal dock can still be seen.

Along the remote portions of the line many section houses still stand, some having been re-designated as "stations." Where stops are needed to disembark passengers heading for cottages or for wilderness canoeing, there are also shelters and umbrella stations.

While the ACR and the T&NO became the only lines in Ontario to link north with south, three major railway lines crossed northern Ontario from east to west. These were the Canadian Pacific Railway, the Canadian Northern Railway, conceived by Mackenzie and Mann, and the National Transcontinental Railway, Sir Wilfrid Laurier's grand dream.

THE CANADIAN PACIFIC RAILWAY (CPR)

The first railway to cross Ontario's difficult and rocky northland was the CPR. After a delay that followed its groundbreaking in Westfort William in 1875, it completed its link by 1886. With no towns to precede it other than scattered Cree and Ojibwa settlements, the CPR had to create their towns from scratch. With the arrival of the highway network of the 1960s, these communities evolved from trackside villages to highway towns. Nearly the entire roster of the CPR's way stations has gone, however there remains a solid collection of its divisional stations, most remaining in railway use.

MATTAWA

In the summer of 2012, the Canadian Pacific Railway (CPR) got the green light to lift its tracks between Pembroke and Mattawa, a section of rail line that marked the beginning of the CPR's push to the Pacific. By 1881, the site marked the CPR's head of rail. Despite the demise of the Ottawa Valley line, trains continue to haul timber from the massive mills in Temiscaming, Quebec.

The station itself dates from 1902 and displays an extended version of a common CPR storey-and-a-half style with a bell-cast roof and both front and rear hip dormers. While the main station is wood-on-stone, a later freight shed extension to the east is simple frame. As of 2012, the building is boarded up, although a communications tower still stands.

NORTH BAY

As the Canadian Pacific Railway (CPR) was laying its tracks to the Pacific, it chose a location on Lake Nipissing to place the divisional point of North Bay, consisting of engine shop, roundhouse, and large wooden station. In 1902, as part of its initiative to upgrade the stations along the Ottawa Valley, the CPR replaced the earlier building with a two-storey stone station with both red and grey stonework, and a single-storey extension, which gained a second storey in the 1940s.

Passenger service ended in 1990 and the CPR itself subsequently vacated the structure. While the tracks remain in use, the building has become a "discovery" centre and museum.

SUDBURY

The next surviving station west of North Bay is that at Sudbury. Although the separate office building was removed in the late 1990s, the single-storey station has survived. Built in1907 as part of a station replacement program, the brick on stone station featured a steep bell-cast roofline with a dormer in the roof to accommodate the station agent. Although the dormer is now gone, the station remains the point of departure for VIA Rail's *Superior* train to White River.

CARTIER

One hundred and fifty kilometres northwest of Sudbury, the Canadian Pacific Railway carved the divisional town of Cartier into the northern bush. The two-storey wooden Cartier station was built in 1910 and doubled in size in 1948. A pair of dormers in the roof originally accommodated the agent's quarters as well as the railway offices. The railway continues to use the station and the yards.

CHAPLEAU

Chapleau was laid out as a divisional headquarters of the Canadian Pacific Railway (CPR) and remains a major rail divisional point. Here it retains repair shops and is a crew change for the freight trains. A small waiting room in the CPR's modern flat-roofed station, the third on the site, offers space for VIA passengers.

WHITE RIVER

Like Cartier, White River was created by the Canadian Pacific Railway (CPR) as a major divisional point for its operations. It is much quieter now, with only a small bunkhouse for the crew. The station structures are not original, the main two-storey brick office structure dates from 1947, while the single-storey, international-style station, also brick, was added in 1957. Although VIA still calls, the station sees little use.

SCHREIBER

Located halfway between White River and Thunder Bay, Schreiber was, like Chapleau, a major divisional headquarters for the Canadian Pacific Railway (CPR). Although downgraded to divisional point, it remains a crew-change location with a number of functions still operating out of the long two-storey station. Built in 1924, following a fire that destroyed the earlier building, the station offers a much simpler design, with its long, two-storey, brick-on-concrete construction and hipped roof. Gabled dormers extend above the eaves over the second and eighth bays, with an extended canopy along the platform. With the end of passenger service in 1990, the restaurant and waiting rooms were converted into more functional space for the train crews.

THUNDER BAY

Thunder Bay not only remains a hub of railway and shipping activity, it was also where "the west began." It was on the banks of the Kaministiquia River, not far from the old fur trading post of Fort William, that the Canadian Pacific Railway (CPR) broke ground for its construction along the Lake Superior shore. A small station was erected and yards were laid out. But as shipping boomed, the CPR shifted its major yards closer to the grain elevators and, jointly with the Grand Trunk Pacific in 1910, opened a new union station. The three-storey, flat-topped brick building includes a row of pilasters and a stone arch above the street entrance, which is flanked by decorative friezes depicting sheaves of wheat.

KENORA

Early on, the Canadian Pacific Railway recognized the tourist potential of the land through which it was built. Not only was the location on Lake of the Woods important to supply water for its divisional point, but the beauty of its waters and islands brought tourists, and so in 1899 the railway opened another of its Château-style stations. Constructed of brick, the two-storey station displays a Château-style roofline with several hip-gables and dormers, as well as a tower over the front entrance. The flower gardens and fountain, which once adorned the street side, have given way to parking. Gone too is the Railway YMCA which housed the train crews. Passenger service ended in 1990. The Kenricia Hotel, built to accommodate arriving tourists, still stands. Designed by Chicago architect Frank Newell, the beaux-arts style hotel opened its doors in 1910.

THE NATIONAL TRANSCONTINENTAL RAILWAY: SIR WILFRID'S DREAM

With the completion of Laurier's National Transcontinental Railway across the far northern reaches of Ontario in 1913, the railway erected a string of look-alike stations. The structures for the stations in these towns and villages were single-storey with a small dormer tucked into an upstairs bell-cast roof for the agent. None survive as stations. Only that at Opasatika still stands and is now a Caisse Populaire.

The divisional stations were similarly simple — a full two storeys with hip-gables at each end and occasionally a prominent gable in the middle. Such divisional stations were built at Hearst, Armstrong, Redditt, Sioux Lookout, and Nakina, those at Armstrong, Redditt, and Hearst now gone.

KAPUSKASING

In 1913, the NTR built one of its standard-plan rural stations on the west bank of the Kapuskasing River, at that time known as McPherson. But in 1923, when the Spruce Falls Pulp and Paper Company built its new pulp mills and created a modern townsite called Kapuskasing, the CNR, the NTR's successor, added an attractive Richardsonian Romanesque brick station near the new town on the east side of the river. The operator's bay, with its three-paned arched window, extends through the roofline to a Flemish-style gable. The bell-cast roof extends over the platform. A freight room extends the building to the west. With the cancelling of passenger service in 1990 the building became a tourist office and bus depot.

NAKINA

Similarly, that at Nakina, built in 1923 by the CNR, has also been retained and has become a multi-modal facility, where VIA's *Canadian* comes calling two or three times a week. This two-storey structure is constructed of wood on a stone base with single-storey wings at each end. An extended overhang wraps around the entire lower level.

SIOUX LOOKOUT

The NTR's two-storey Sioux Lookout station displayed a little more decorative imagination, with cross-gables at each end and a Tudoresque half-timbered design. In 2007, the Town of Sioux Lookout bought the station to restore it as a component of its downtown revitalization plan.

The CNR replaced many of the NTR's first-generation rural stations with those similar to that at Minaki. A boxy two-storey pattern, it now houses a gift shop and remains a stopping point for VIA Rail. The area is popular with cottagers from Winnipeg, many of whom travel to the area by rail. The CNR added smaller stations, primarily shelters for the cottagers, including those at Ottermere and Malachi which remain but neither is road accessible.

MACKENZIE AND MANN CONQUER THE NORTH

A short distance to the east of North Bay's former Canadian Pacific Railway (CPR) station stands the revitalized former Canadian Northern (CNo) station. In 1914, as William Mackenzie and Donald Mann were adding to their cross-country network with a link from Capreol to Ottawa, they assigned their eastern architect, George Briggs, to design a grand station for North Bay. Influenced by the Romanesque station designs of American H.H. Richardson, Briggs incorporated into the brick and stone building arched entrances at both the street and track sides, while chandeliers lit the vaulted waiting room. After sitting vacant and vandalized following the Canadian National Railway's departure, the building has gained new life as the Crisis Centre North Bay.

Between North Bay and Thunder Bay most of the CNo stations were subsequently replaced by the Canadian National Railway (CNR) and have since been removed, as have the tracks between Pembroke and Capreol, and between Longlac and Thunder Bay, much to the resentment of local businesses, which relied upon the service. Rail still remains between Capreol and Longlac. The CNR station still stands in Hornepayne, a divisional point selected by the CNo. Although designated, and despite efforts by the CNR to find a local saviour, the otherwise solid brick, two-storey building is nearing a state of ruin.

RAINY RIVER COUNTRY

When the Canadian Northern acquired its link from Manitoba into Ontario via Rainy River in 1901, it built a string of its standard pyramid-roof, prairie-style stations. A few, such as those which stood in Barwick and Stratton, rest now on private lands. The Silver Mountain station, on a proposed Duluth branch, still on its original now-trackless site, has become a popular restaurant featuring "Silver Mountain chicken."

FORT FRANCES

The Fort Frances station still stands on-site as well. Although the main portion displays the typical Canadian Northern Railway (CNo) pyramid roof, long extensions at each end reflect its additional roles as divisional point and customs entry point for trains crossing from International Falls, Minnesota.

Constructed of wood, the building now houses the Fort Frances Volunteer Bureau.

RAINY RIVER

Rainy River, a divisional town situated on the Rainy River, was another international point of entry from Minnesota. The Canadian Northern Railway's station here was more typical of their Ontario divisional stations made of brick, with a prominent cross-gable over the entrance and operators' bay. Two dormers in the roof rest on either side of it. It was built in 1918, near the end of the CNo's corporate existence, and now houses municipal offices.

PORT ARTHUR

Now Thunder Bay, the former city of Port Arthur offers the finest station that the Canadian Northern Railway (CNo) built anywhere in the country. Here R.B. Pratt designed a pair of three-storey towers topped with the iconic pyramid roof. On each side of the peak are dormers which themselves contains rows of windows. Above the windows stone friezes depicting sheaves of wheat recount the railway's role as one of Canada's leading grain shippers. Small circular towers appear at the four corners of the larger roof towers. The end towers are linked by a storey-and-a-half central section with a prominent cross-gable. The brick building has several stone highlights around the windows and doorways. The extravagance in its design reflected its vital role as a port of entry for the many arriving ships and their cargo of tourists and business magnates.

Despite its ornate architecture, the interior was built to be more functional, containing waiting rooms, customs offices, an elegant dining room, and freight room. No train has stopped here in years and the tracks were lifted prior to 2010. The building is now part of a major waterfront revitalization and, although vacant in 2012, will be an office for nearby condos, meaning much of the interior will be restored to its earlier grandeur and a restaurant may be added.

The CNo's former Port Arthur station in Thunder Bay is railway architect R.B. Pratt's finest creation.

— 4 —

SAVING OUR STATIONS:

NEW USES FOR OLD STATIONS

Once the railways no longer need a station, the buildings become a liability and are quickly demolished, with the attitude of "the sooner the better." During the late 1970s and early 1980s, under the presidency of Ian Sinclair, the Canadian Pacific Railway (CPR) went on a demolition frenzy and removed nearly all their Ontario station buildings, costing many towns and villages one of their most important heritage structures. The Canadian National Railway (CNR) was almost as thorough.

Ironically, it was this era of cultural vandalism by the railways that led to the rescue of many of Canada's remaining stations.

In 1982, in the midst of negotiations to save the CPR's historic Tudoresque station at West Toronto Junction, the railway sent in a wrecking crew during the night and by dawn the building was rubble. The courts eventually absolved the CPR of wrong-doing, but the incident awoke Canadians to the fate of these cherished buildings.

Later, in 1988, the House of Commons enacted legislation known as the Heritage Railway Station Protection Act to protect redundant railway stations from such wanton demolition. It was the only private members' bill to gain unanimous consent in the House of Commons. Once in the Senate, the CPR's ex-president, Sinclair, tried to rally opposition to the act, but failed. His vote was the only one cast against it.

Across the country more than three hundred stations were designated under the new law, over

Although federally "protected," the GT's historic first-generation 1856 station in Ernestown shows obvious signs of neglect and vandalism. It is a rare surviving example of that line's "Kenilworth" station type.

Although federally designated, the ACR station in Searchmont deteriorates while awaiting a local saviour.

fifty in Ontario alone. However, if no local group offered to undertake re-use of these buildings, the railways simply left them to rot or burn down. And many did.

In addition to those stations so designated, dozens more have been saved and carted away to become museums, garages, restaurants, and private homes. A few recycled stations remain on their original grounds.

MOUNT PLEASANT

While it is barely noticeable from the road, the attractive Mount Pleasant station, southwest of Brantford, rests only a few metres from its original site on the Lake Erie and Northern Railway. It was built in 1916 using one of the Canadian Pacific Railway's more common storey-and-a-half styles. It retains its original coat of CPR Tuscan-red paint with yellow highlights.

BRANTFORD

Although they are now only occasionally used, tracks still pass by the 1896 TH&B station in Brantford. Vacant in 2012, the brick-on-stone station, with its two dormers in the roof, has operated on and off as a restaurant.

SOUTHAMPTON

The 1906 Grand Trunk (GT) station in Southampton is surrounded now by newer development but has served as a restaurant known as Trax and, later, Grosvenors'. This delightful brick station offers a sheltered porch over the street entrance and a high gable above the bay on what was once the trackside.

WIARTON

The white, wooden former Wiarton station now stands in Bluewater Park, refurbished and now serving as a park centre. Having been a "terminal" station, it boasts a few extra architectural features including a rounded waiting room and a small tower.

PETROLIA AND THE OIL FIELDS

With the discovery of oil in southwestern Ontario in 1858, the railways were not far behind. The Grand Trunk (GT) extended a branch from its main Sarnia line south into Petrolia, then the oil capital of Canada. Similarly the Canada Southern extended a branch northward from its own main line located to the south of the town.

The elegant brick three-towered Petrolia GT station, which faces the main street, has been a library for half a century, while the wooden CASO station, with its corner tower, was split in two to become dwellings on the shores of Lake St. Clair. Down on the CASO's main line, the Oil Springs station, a simple, American-style board-and-batten building, sits now on the grounds of the Oil Springs Museum located at the site of North America's first commercial oil well. Further west, the CASO Mooretown station similarly rests on a local museum grounds.

GLENCOE

Although smaller than its other towered stations, the Grand Trunk (GT) station in Glencoe also fell in with the tower craze of the late 1890s and early 1900s. Built in 1904, it features an octagonal tower above the octagonal waiting room. The remaining features were, however, rather standard with a gable over the bay and bell-cast roof with wraparound overhang. Following the closure of the building by

Glencoe's GT station shows how a community can protect and celebrate its railway heritage.

CN Rail, the community took over, moved it a short distance back from the track, and converted it into a combined museum and event venue. It retains its high ceilings, where the waiting room is now a boardroom for the local Rotary, while the agents' office displays historic photos and railway artifacts.

ORANGEVILLE

As a key divisional point on the Toronto, Grey and Bruce Railway (TG&B), later the Canadian Pacific Railway (CPR), Orangeville warranted a grander station, and it got it. In 1906 the CPR replaced the simpler TG&B station with a plan known as the "witch's hat," a rounded waiting room with a conical roof. A separate building housed the usual divisional point dining room. When the CPR threatened to demolish the wood-shingled station, a restaurateur moved the building closer to the downtown and opened the Station Bar and Grill. The Orangeville Brampton Railway opened a new tourist station on the old site after the dining room building burned in 2006.

PORT COLBORNE

The town in 1833 became the southern terminus of the newly opened Welland Canal. In 1854, the Buffalo, Brantford and Goderich Railway, later the Buffalo and Lake Huron Railway, crossed the canal and opened a station on the east side. By the 1920s the CNR owned the line and added a large brick station on the west side at the junction of the Niagara, St. Catharines, and Toronto Street Railway, which linked Port Dalhousie with Port Colborne. Built in an era when simplicity was the goal, the large brick station has few embellishments other that a hip dormer above the bay. It is now a restaurant and contains offices of the Trillium Railway, a short-line operation.

Displaying extra detailing in its fretwork, the TH&B station in Smithville now serves as a community archives and tourist office.

SMITHVILLE

This is another one of those small architectural gems that local efforts have managed to save. It was built in 1893 by the Toronto, Hamilton and Buffalo Railway (later CPR) with a decorative tower rising above the waiting room. The wooden white and green station displays an unusual amount of decorative wood trim in the gable above the bay and around the upper part of the turret. It now rests a few metres back from the tracks and houses the West Lincoln Historical Society archives, as well as a tourist information office in the restored waiting room.

OTTERVILLE

In 1876 the Port Dover and Lake Huron Railway constructed their line from Port Dover to Stratford and built a string of simple, single-storey, board-and-batten stations, that in Otterville being the sole survivor. In 1991, the South Norfolk Historical Society relocated the building from its original site where it had been used for storage, to the museum grounds at the west end of the village. Here it was repainted to its early two-tone green paint scheme, while a historical display was created inside.

TILLSONBURG

This bustling town in the middle of Ontario's dwindling tobacco country was home to several lines including the Canadian Pacific Railway (CPR), the Great Western (GW), and the Canada Southern(CASO). In 1876, the latter built a standard single-storey station on its line at the north end of town. Located on Tillson Street, with tracks gone, it is now professional offices.

In the heart of Tillsonburg's downtown the Great Western Railway built its station in 1879. The solid brick building features a steep roof and prominent gables. Here too the tracks have long since been removed, and following fifteen years of restoration work it now houses the Tillsonburg Arts Centre. Next to it stands yet another station, that formerly owned by the CPR and located on King Street. It was relocated adjacent to the GW station in 1992, where it is currently a daycare.

KINGSVILLE

The impetus for the attractive stone station in the lakeside town of Kingsville originated with the Windsor distillery magnate Hiram Walker, who had built the Lake Erie and Detroit River Railway to Lake Erie in order to haul raw material for his Windsor operation. In 1888 he recognized the tourism potential of Kingsville and commissioned Albert Kahn to design the station.

Like that in Essex, the station was built of stone in the Richardsonian Romanesque style, with its rounded tower, porte cochère, and prominent arched windows and entrances. The station also featured a rare slate roof. In near-ruin during the 1980s, and now a designated heritage structure, it has been restored and is a prominent feature on the Chrysler Canada Greenway, which follows the railbed through Essex County. The Mettawas Restaurant opened in the station in 2008.

AMHERSTBURG

In 1872, it had been the intention of CASO to bridge the Detroit River north of Amherstburg at Gordon Station. Although the bridge was never built, trains crossed on ferries to the Michigan Central line south of Detroit. In 1883, a more direct link via Windsor replaced the Amherstburg line, which was reduced to a branch line. In 1895, a new brick station opened in downtown Amherstburg. Measuring 10 metres by 25 metres, the building featured dressed stone window sills and fan lights above the windows. In 1969, Florence Gibson bought the then-redundant building and donated it to the Fort Malden Guild of Arts and Crafts, which operates it today as the Gibson Gallery. Landscaping has replaced any evidence of the once-busy tracks.

BRAMPTON CPR

This decorative brick, single-storey station was built in 1907 by the Canadian Pacific Railway (CPR) on what had been its Credit Valley line. In 1977, declared redundant by the CPR, it was cut in half and moved to a nursery where it remained until 1995, when it was dismantled and put in storage. Then, in 2010 the City of Brampton reassembled the building as part of a community centre complex close to the Mount Pleasant GO station west of the urban area.

ELDON/BRECHIN

In 1911, when the Canadian Pacific Railway (CPR) opened its Georgian Bay and Seaboard line from Dranoel near Lindsay to Port McNicoll, it erected a string of stations using a then-current standard plan which included a two-storey, pyramid-roofed building with dormers to accommodate the agents' quarters, and single-storey extensions to accommodate freight and passenger traffic. Following the closing of the line in 1937, two stations were sold and today remain onsite. That in Brechin, with the addition of railway equipment, was the Wild Wings Restaurant in 2012, while that at Eldon, north of Argyle, became a private home.

JERSEYVILLE

Now under the care of the Westfield Heritage Village in Rockton near Hamilton, the former TH&B station from Jerseyville represents a typical American-style station. Single-storey and constructed of wood, it features gable ends and a gable above the operator's bay. The interior offers a glimpse of station life in the 1950s and is accompanied by steam locomotive 103, built for the TH&B in 1918.

KING CITY — CANADA'S OLDEST?

This simple structure, which lies on the grounds of the King Township Museum with a grouping of local heritage buildings, may well be the oldest surviving station in Canada. It was built by the Ontario, Simcoe, and Huron Railway, Ontario's first steam-powered railway, in 1853. Most stations along the line were of the same style: board-and-batten, single-storey, the eave extended over the platform, the windows were arched, and a small gable indented the roofline. After languishing in a local conservation area, it was moved to the museum grounds where it has been restored and repainted in green and grey.

LOCUST HILL

This small Canadian Pacific Railway (CPR) station from Locust Hill rests within the Markham Heritage Museum village. Built in 1936 by the CPR, it replaced a "Van Horne" station of the kind that lined the Ontario and Quebec Railway from Toronto to Smiths Falls. This standard CPR pattern-book building is typical of the period, with few architectural embellishments. The building is single-storey and wooden, with a shallow pitched roof and a simple wraparound overhang. Sitting on a track by the platform is a 1921 CN Rail passenger coach, the *Acadia*.

SUTTON

The Georgina Pioneer Village near Sutton has managed to acquire three stations for its display. A rare surviving pair of shelters from the Toronto and York Radial Railway (TYRR) sit in the grounds with their open façade and tile roofs. (Another TYRR shelter was found in a Thornhill garden and returned to near its original location on Yonge Street, south of the former village of Thornhill.) The museum grounds also contain the restored 1920 CN Rail station from the nearby village of Sutton. It reflects the simplicity that the newly formed Canadian National Railway (CNR) was applying to its new or replacement stations, namely wooden with a wide, shallow pitched roof, with hip-gables at the ends and a wraparound eave. Other relocated stations in the area include the 1909 Canadian Northern (CNo) station from Richmond Hill to Richmond Green on Elgin Mills Road, and the 1909 CNo station from Mount Albert to the grounds of the Cannington Centennial Museum in McLeod Park.

MIMICO

In 2007, volunteers dragged what was Toronto's last wooden station, the Mimico station, across the street to Coronation Park on Royal York Road to undergo restoration. The simple single-storey structure features hip-gable ends and a gable above the operators' bay. It dates to 1915, when it was built by the Grand Trunk shortly after opening the adjacent New Toronto yards.

WHITBY

Built in 1901 as part of the Grand Trunk's upgrading program, this attractive wooden station was given two octagonal towers on the track side and one at the street entrance. The towers stood above a pair of octagonal bay windows and were topped by steep bell-cast roofs.

The station marked the all-important junction between the Grand Trunk (GT) and the Whitby, Port Perry, and Lindsay Railway. By 1969, CN Rail had ended its passenger service and planned to demolish the building. That was when the Whitby arts community relocated the station to the corner of Henry and Victoria Streets, converting it to an art gallery and adding a boxcar to enhance the railway ambience. In 2005, now repainted in the GT green-and-grey paint scheme, it was moved once more to its current location at the Iroquois Park Sports Complex, where it was also enlarged to accommodate additional display space.

PETERSBURG

Built in 1856, the Grand Trunk's Petersburg station reflects a forgotten GT pattern, with only a few being erected west of Kitchener. The small wooden building with unusual rooflines and gables has resided in the Doon Heritage Village, now part of the Waterloo Regional Museum, since 1968, with Canadian Pacific Railway steam engine #894 in front.

HARROW

This interesting Canadian Transportation Museum and Heritage Village depicts many aspects of Canada's transportation heritage. Several historical automobiles lie in the museum building, while the heritage village includes the Grand Trunk's

Tecumseh station, moved to the grounds in 1974. The single-storey wooden building includes a gable above the operator's bay window and a second peaked gable at the end. A small Buffalo and South Western Railway diesel #800 and a caboose rest beside the building.

CALEDONIA

With tracks still in front, the 1913 Grand Trunk station in Caledonia has been carefully restored and authentically repainted and now houses the Caledonia Chamber of Commerce along with historic displays. The single-storey wooden building contains a stepped roof that heightens over the central waiting room. A former freight shed extends to the west. Tracks are leased to the Southern Ontario Railway, a short-line that serves a pair of local industries as well as the factories at Nanticoke on Lake Erie.

JARVIS

The station in this community displays a number of interesting features. Constructed of wood by the Grand Trunk in 1906, it served both the Canada Air Line and the Hamilton and Northwestern lines, which had their tracks on opposite sides of the building. Both later became part of the Canadian

National Railway. As a result, operator's bay windows are located on both sides of the station. The bays and the gables above them are octagonal, as is the former waiting room at the western end of the structure. Tracks have long since been lifted and the station, as of 2012, houses Michaud Fine Woodworking.

HALIBURTON

Chartered in 1874, George Laidlaw's proposed Fenelon Falls and Ottawa Valley Railway failed to make it beyond Haliburton and was renamed the Victoria Railway. It reached Haliburton in 1878, where the Victoria Railway erected a wooden station. With its board-and-batten wood trim, and a gable above the bay, it was a small but attractive structure. Today it has been placed on a higher foundation and, with tracks gone, it is home to the Haliburton Highlands Guild of Fine Arts.

KINMOUNT

The former Victoria Railway has a few stations left to celebrate. Similar to that in Haliburton, with its use of gables and board-and-batten exterior, that in Kinmount also has a new life as home to the Kinmount Model Railway and Museum, as well as a tourist information office. The building remains on its original site, with the railway roadbed now a rail trail.

FENELON FALLS

Although surrounded by newer development, with the old right-of-way no longer evident, the Fenelon Falls station on the Victoria Railway (VR) has been carefully restored with its arched Italianate-style windows. The simple wooden building now houses the Chamber of Commerce. The station was built in 1882 by the Midland Railway, which absorbed the VR before itself becoming part of the Grand Trunk.

COBOCONK

Located at the terminus of the truncated Toronto and Nipissing Railway (ironically, it got nowhere near Nipissing) in Coboconk, the original station burned before 1900 and was replaced by the Grand Trunk station. The wooden board-and-batten building, single-storey at one end and two-storey at the other, was moved to the Rotary Park where it is gradually being restored.

GODERICH

Despite damage to many of its heritage buildings in a deadly 2011 tornado, Goderich retains a grand railway-station heritage, with a pair of Ontario's most attractive stations. The Canadian Pacific Railway (CPR) station was built in 1907, close to the busy harbour, and was designed to attract tourists as well. This brick-on-stone building incorporates Richardsonian-style doors, windows, and arches, as well as a dominating witch's hat roof above the rounded waiting room. Rounded arches mark the operators' bay while a porte cochère welcomes travellers at the entrance. All windows are topped by limestone lintels. A second set of windows around the upper section of the waiting room add to the illumination of the wooded interior. After the tracks were lifted in 1987, the town acquired the building, using it for exhibits and events. As of 2012, a proposal has been advanced to move the building closer to the water and convert it to a restaurant. One hopes that the exterior elements remain in place.

In addition to that of the CPR, Goderich enjoys a second station gem as well. It lies inland and was designed in 1902 by the Grand Trunk's architect N.G. Batten and replaced an earlier Buffalo and Lake Huron station. The brick station, built in a Château style, is marked by two towers on the street side. The door is topped with an arch while a wide eave wraps around the entire structure. Although the station now has professional tenants, the track remains used by the Goderich and Exeter Railway.

WINGHAM

This squat, boxy building is a rather unusual looking structure. Marking the street entrance at the end of the station are two square unadorned towers that were twice their current height when first built. With tracks on both sides, the station also featured two bay windows on opposite sides of the building, both octagonal, which rise to octagonal dormers set into the roof. After lying derelict following the track removal, it has been renovated and is now a municipal office. The station was built by the Grand Trunk in 1906, replacing the original Wellington, Grey, and Bruce station.

CRAIGLEITH

This attractive, turreted station was built in 1881 by the Northern Railway, an extension of Ontario's oldest rail line, the Ontario, Simcoe, and Huron Railway ("Oats Straw and Hay" to its earlier travellers), which opened between Toronto and Allandale in 1853. In 1872, the line was extended to Meaford. In 1888, both the Northern Railway and the Hamilton and Northwestern Railway were taken over by the expanding Grand

Trunk. Not only did the Craigleith station handle the usual lumber and farm products, but as the Blue Mountains became a mecca for skiers, the ski trains became a common sight and ran to Craigleith as often as six times a day.

But the Canadian National Railway, which had assumed control of the Grand Trunk in 1923, ended passenger service in 1960 and announced that the station would be demolished. In 1966, Ken Knapman rescued the empty building, opening The Depot restaurant two years later. In 2001, with demolition threats being raised, this time by condo developers, the Town of Blue Mountain rescued the building. After years of fundraising, the Craigleith Heritage Committee and the Blue Mountain Waterfront Trust Foundation raised enough funds to open the Craigleith Heritage Museum. The rail line, now the Georgian Trail, is popular with hikers and cyclists.

OWEN SOUND

Stations of both the Canadian National Railway (CNR) and Canadian Pacific Railway (CPR) yet stand in Owen Sound. In 1884, the Grand Trunk extended a branch into Owen Sound from its Wiarton line at Park Head junction. On the west side of the harbour it built the line's first station. In 1932, the CNR replaced the earlier structure with a single-storey station featuring a prominent cross-gable over the operators' bay and street entrance. After trains stopped coming in 1970, the station became a museum with tracks and a boxcar out front. A hiking trail follows the former right-of-way to the Park Head junction.

Across the harbour stands the vacant CPR station. Built following the Second World War in 1946, the building replaced an earlier Toronto, Grey and Bruce station with an international style featuring a single-storey, flat roof and generous windows. Art deco features include the free-standing aluminum lettering, a flat wrap-around overhang, and a concrete column above one corner. Amid much controversy (which continues today) the tracks were lifted in the 1990s and the station remains vacant.

WATERLOO

Today, Waterloo can claim two stations. The older of the two was built in 1910 by the Grand Trunk to replace an earlier Waterloo Central Railway building constructed on this branch line to Elmira in 1891. The yellow brick building in downtown Waterloo is distinguished by slender arched windows and an arched entrance on the end that accesses the street. The triangular cross-gable rises above the operators' bay window. Since closing, it has housed a variety of retail uses. The station's original tracks remain in place.

The newer of the two stations marks the terminus of the Waterloo Southern Railway, formerly the Waterloo and St. Jacobs Railway, and was designed to resemble a typical Grand Trunk station: wooden with board-and-batten siding, gable, and a porte cochère to shelter waiting passengers. Passengers board here for a short journey on heritage coaches to the St. Jacobs Farmers' Market or the village of St. Jacobs itself. Its future is jeopardized by a municipal proposal for a controversial Light Rail Transit line.

WOLVERTON

Now resting on the Drumbo fairgrounds is the 1881 Canadian Pacific Railway (CPR) station from Wolverton. Built in a simple CPR pattern on what was the Credit Valley Railway, it served ignominiously as a farm outbuilding until the Drumbo and District Heritage Society rescued it and, with the help of a grant from the CPR, restored it to its original maroon and yellow paint scheme. Like many of that pattern, including that in the Markham heritage museum, it is single-storey, wood, and has a wraparound overhanging eave. It was built in 1913.

PALMERSTON

The grand old station that sits in what was once a busy divisional yard is another example of community work. The original portion of the station was built by the Wellington, Grey, and Bruce Railway in 1872, adding the second storey in 1876. After the Grand Trunk (GT) acquired the line in 1882, it added two towers at the east end and a semicircular waiting room. As did all GT lines, that through Palmerston became part of the Canadian National Railway (CNR), which removed many of the station's more elegant features. After the CN vacated the station, it sat empty until 1996 when the Town of Palmerston bought the building and the surrounding yards. The local community, and especially the Lions Club, embarked upon a renovation that restored the original exterior by stripping away the insulbrick and restoring the wood trim with its green and grey paint scheme. Much of the interior is restored as well, and today houses a museum. It also hosts the annual hard cart races which use the remaining track in the yard.

The Allandale GT station in Barrie, restored by the city, is Ontario's largest and most attractive wooden station.

HARRISTON

Also on its original site is the Grand Trunk's elegant 1905 Harriston station, which replaced an 1871 Wellington, Grey, and Bruce station. Now a seniors' drop-in centre, the brick station displays a stepped bell-cast roof, an octagonal roof covering the operator's octagonal bay, and a prominent gable on its roof. This heritage building typifies the line's grander station styles in Midwestern Ontario.

LAKEFIELD

Still on its original site in Lakefield, the appealing little Grand Trunk station was built in 1907. Single-storey and built of wood, the building features prominent gables and marks the location of the Lakefield Rail Trail which follows the Trent-Severn Waterway to Peterborough. In 2012, it was a popular used book store.

ALLANDALE

Considered to be Ontario's largest wooden station, and one of its more attractive, the station at Allandale, now a part of Barrie, was added in 1905 by the Grand Trunk after it acquired the Northern and Northwestern Railway. The site was a major junction and divisional point. The station consists of three sections: a brick office structure; a wooden pillared portion in the centre, which housed the restaurant; and the rounded waiting room, which occupied the eastern end of the building where the passengers could enjoy a vista across Lake Simcoe.

Above the waiting room windows rested a crown-like canopy, and, in the style of the day, a tower. With many of its patrons being wealthy Muskoka cottagers and lodge visitors, the dining hall boasted high windows, uniformed staff, and seating for fifty. The City of Barrie, which acquired the building after years of intermittent ownership, totally restored the elegant structure, completing the work in 2012. A new GO station close by has brought rail travel back close to the doors of the grand old station.

ORILLIA

Ignoring local outrage, and despite having just installed new rail, the CNR lifted the tracks between Barrie and Orillia. Happily, they left the Orillia station in place.

It was here that two important rail lines crossed — the Northern and Pacific Junction Railway and the Midland Railway, each originally with their own stations. By 1888, the Grand Trunk (GT) had taken over both and built a common station. But by 1914, with ridership increasing, the GT replaced the older structure with a grand, new brick building. The building features textured stonework around the windows and a stone base. The stepped roof includes a hip-gable over the operator's bay. Tracks passed on each side of the building.

All tracks are gone now and the building serves as a government office and bus depot. But the city of Orillia would have been far better served had rail passenger service remained. With GO trains now extended to Barrie, that opportunity has been lost.

PARRY SOUND

As with Goderich, the Georgian Bay town of Parry Sound has held onto its two train stations. And, as with Goderich, that of the Canadian Pacific Railway was built in 1908 using the eclectic "witch's hat" style. The wood shingle siding of the Parry Sound station has been repainted to its original yellow and maroon scheme, while inside most of the interior remains intact, including a curved wooden bench

The CPR's Parry Sound station, now a community building, displays the "witch's hat" style added by the CPR to attract tourists.

in the waiting room. Though VIA Rail's north-bound *Canadian* still stops there, the structure is today owned by the town and used for a variety of municipal events.

A short distance away, the Canadian National Railway (CNR) station also survives. Built by the CNR, it replaced the Canadian Northern's divisional station, which stood on the opposite side of the Seguin River. Here too, the *Canadian* halts on its southbound leg where a small waiting room houses passengers. The rest of the building's interior has been modernized to house the Chamber of Commerce office. The building, built in the late 1920s, is yellow brick on a concrete foundation and features a prominent cross-gable over the entrance and operator's bay.

KINGSTON

In 1875 Kingston's waterfront was a far different place than it is today. Parks, hotels, and condos have replaced what up until the 1970s was a landscape of wharfs, mills, and the railway sidings of the Kingston and Pembroke Railway (by then the Canadian Pacific Railway). Some rail heritage remains. Most prominent is the CPR's former Kingston and Pembroke station. Built of local limestone and with a slate bell-cast roof and a row of arched windows reminiscent of the Grand Trunk's first stations, it now functions as a tourist information office. In front rests the

steam locomotive, known as the Spirit of Sir John A., which carried the body of Sir John A. Macdonald to be buried at Cataraque. Built in 1885 by the CPR, the station replaced the original Kingston and Pembroke Railway station which had been there for a decade.

While Kingston's "outer" Grand Trunk (GT) station crumbles, the city has a second surviving GT station. On Ontario Street, Frankie Pesto's Restaurant occupied what began as the GT's "inner" station. Built of brick with a mansard roof and corner entrance, it marked the 1886 terminus of the GT's branch line that connected downtown Kingston with its "outer" station several kilometres away on the main line.

STIRLING

One of Ontario's more outstanding jobs at celebrating and preserving a station was that undertaken in Stirling. It represents the last example of a Canadian Pacific Railway "Van Horne" station even though it was built in 1879 by the Grand Junction Railway. It continued to operate until 1962 and then stood vacant until 2005 when the Rotary Club, the historical society, and the municipality moved the structure onto a new foundation, adding a new basement meeting room and installing a station museum in the first and second floors. The roadbed is now a trail.

THE BOQ STRING

It is unusual for a railway company to leave an entire string of stations, but the stations which line the roadbed of the former Bay of Quinte Railway are a happy exception. In 1879 Edward Rathbun launched the Nappanee, Tamworth, and Quebec Railway from Deseronto, later to become the Bay of Quinte Railway. In 1889 the line was extended to Bannockburn where it met the Central Ontario Railway. Along the line the BOQ built a string of nearly identical stations. Two-storeys in height, they displayed a bay window which extended to the second floor, allowing the agent to monitor train traffic from his quarters. After the tracks were lifted in the 1940s, the stations were sold. Today they remain on their original sites between Napanee and Tweed, and include Newburgh, Tamworth, Erinsville, Marlbank, Stoco, and Queensborough. Little altered, they are now private homes or in the case of that at Erinsville, a municipal storage facility.

MAYNOOTH

A small community in remote central Ontario, Maynooth was the northern terminal for the Central Ontario Railway (although tracks did extend a few kilometres north of that), built from Trenton to northern Hastings County. As such, it contained a second floor with the railway's offices. The building is a simple style with few architectural embellishments and the yards also contained a water tower and roundhouse. Having been abandoned for three decades, the mighty two-storey concrete structure needs work, which is why as of 2012 a dedicated group of local volunteers are raising funds to stabilize the roof. The rest of the structure remains solid.

BANCROFT

This too was a fine station on the Central Ontario Railway. The wooden building with its steep roof and roofline dormer housed a mineral museum and information office until recently. In 2012, at a cost of more than a half million dollars, the Bancroft and District Chamber of Commerce placed the station on a new foundation and it continues to fundraise for modern requirements such as proper heating, electricity, and an elevator.

Otherwise, the Central Ontario Railway created a string of simple look-alike stations, single-storey with a roof that extended over the platform. Surviving examples have been moved to Coe Hill's fairground, Marmora's riverside park, and from Frankford to a location near Stockdale.

BARRY'S BAY

A unique survivor, the storey-and-a-half wooden station in Barry's Bay is the last of the "Booth Line's" distinctive stations. Booth's standard style incorporated a large cross-gable on the upper storey which extended over the platform. While all other such stations are now gone, that in Barry's Bay has become a museum. To add to the railway heritage of the town, the wooden water tower still stands as well.

CARLETON PLACE

In the 1920s the Canadian Pacific Railway (CPR) built a string of attractive stone stations along the Ottawa Valley, situating them in Almonte, Arnprior, Perth, Pembroke, Renfrew, and Carleton Place. During the CPR's demolition frenzy of the late 1970s and early 1980s, the railway bulldozed them, despite fierce lobbying by local groups to save them. Only that at Carleton Place survived the destruction. Like the others, it featured stonework all around, with five windows to mark the operator's bay. Following the lifting of the rails of the branch line into Ottawa, the building became a daycare centre and is currently occupied by various tenants.

VARS

In 1975, the Cumberland Heritage Village moved the 1906 Grand Trunk (GT) station from its location in Vars, where it had served passenger trains operating between Ottawa and Montreal. This single-storey wooden building offers a bell-cast roof with peaked hip-gable ends and a gable above the operator's bay window. It has been repainted in the GT's yellow and green paint scheme.

AULTSVILLE

Seemingly in the middle of nowhere along the Thousand Islands Parkway, a station and steam engine appear in the middle of a field. This is the Aultsville Grand Trunk station, rescued when in 1956 the waters of the St. Lawrence Seaway overtook the village, covering streets and foundations. A small section of original track has been left in place beside which local volunteers placed the GT's 1889 station. The wooden building reflects a standard Grand Trunk plan with a single-storey and low, wide roof with gable ends. To round out the display they also added an original GT steam locomotive and a pair of historic coaches.

SMITHS FALLS CPR

The Canadian Pacific Railway (CPR) moved out of its 1890 divisional station in the 1990s, indicating its intent to demolish the building. However, the location survived and today remains a divisional point with busy yards. The building is a storey-and-a-half brick-on-stone with a row of windows, which once illuminated the waiting room. It offers few other architectural embellishments. In 2012 VIA Rail moved out of the tiny waiting room and into its own new shelter at the north end of town. The 140-seat Station Theatre now occupies the building.

HAVELOCK

Despite the Canadian Pacific Railway's rush to demolish its heritage, it did leave a couple of fine stations standing in the Peterborough area. That in Havelock, a divisional town, was opened in 1929. The first station was a standard Van Horne style, built on the Ontario and Quebec Railway in 1888. With the opening of an extension to Port McNicoll in 1912, Havelock grew in importance. But by the time the new station had opened, the CPR's new lakeshore route was diverting most of the earlier traffic away from the older route and the role of the town diminished.

Built of yellow brick on a concrete foundation, the station displays a wide bell-cast roof with overhanging eaves. A prominent gable rises above the operator's bay window. After the CPR vacated the station it stood vacant until a restaurant operation moved in, preserving much of the interior elegance, such as the cove ceiling, the terrazzo floors, and much of the woodwork. The building remains a prominent landmark for the highway entrance into the town.

PETERBOROUGH

While most of the Ontario and Quebec (O&Q) stations followed the Van Horne pattern, that in Peterborough was built of yellow brick on a concrete foundation. It features a single-storey with a hip-gable roof and small dormers at the trackside and the ends. Although the canopy that once covered the platform is gone, the building has been renovated and now houses government offices. Designed by Thomas Sorby and built in 1883, it is the Canadian Pacific Railway's oldest Ontario station. An identical station called "Yorkville" stood on the O&Q line on Yonge Street, but was replaced in 1916 by the new North Toronto station.

NORTH TORONTO — TORONTO'S "OTHER" UNION STATION

While Toronto's "other" union station no longer serves the travelling public, it does serve the drinking public.

In 1884, the Ontario and Quebec (O&Q) Railway completed a new line across the north of Toronto and added a station, initially called "Yorkville." But with the increasing congestion at the Grand Trunk's union station on the waterfront, and the interminable delays in building a new one, the Canadian Pacific Railway (CPR), owner of the O&Q, decided it could wait no longer and hired the firm of Darling and Pearson to design a union station of their own, which it would share with the Canadian Northern Railway (CNo) until that line went bankrupt and became part of the CNR.

The building was operational within an incredible two years. But with the completion of the Front Street Union Station in 1927, the CPR began to use that more convenient facility, and by 1930 the North Toronto station was closed to become a beer store, to which a liquor store was later added.

This building incorporated a classical Italianate influence with its three-storey, flat-roofed waiting room and elegant tower. Overlooking an open square, it is reminiscent of an Italian piazza. The marble-lined, three-storey waiting room was illuminated by elegant chandeliers and three-storey arched windows. Through the early 2000s, the tawdry alterations of the early years were removed and the waiting room and exterior have been returned to their early glory.

OTTAWA

By 1895, Ottawa was becoming a major railway hub. Each rail line, however, had its own station, the Bytown and Prescott, the Canada Atlantic, the Canadian Pacific, and the Ottawa and New York railways located stations in different parts of the town. Although J.R. Booth of the Canada Atlantic Railway tried without success to establish a union station, it was ultimately the Grand Trunk (GT) that acquired rights along the Rideau Canal and here, along with the Château Laurier, built Ottawa's Union Station.

Designed by the firm of Ross and MacFarlane, the station opened in June 1912, although the celebration was severely muted by the loss of Charles M. Hays, president of the Grand Trunk, on the *Titanic*.

The grand building is dominated by its elegant Doric pillars on Rideau Street and a high, domed waiting room. Trains stopped calling in 1966 when, as part of an urban revitalization project, Ottawa's downtown tracks were removed and a new station built further from the city core. The station is now a conference centre and, regrettably, is not generally open to the public.

* * *

Ontario displays a number of examples of where private history-conscious individuals have moved stations to their own property and have carefully preserved the integrity of the building's heritage. Such stations include that from Alliston (CPR), relocated to Tottenham; Vine (CNR), south of Barrie; and Jordan Station (GT), across the road from its original location.

Ottawa's grand former Union Station enjoys new use as a convention centre. Its lofty waiting room, however, is now out of bounds to the public.

ST. THOMAS CASO STATION
THE ULTIMATE RESTORATION

After CN Rail shut down the rail operations at the old CASO station in the early 1980s, the enormous station, although designated under protective legislation, began to deteriorate badly. One developer even proposed selling off the bricks.

Happily, however, On Track St. Thomas and the North America Railway Hall of Fame came to the rescue and the building has resumed its former glory. The Ontario and federal governments also contributed, as did the Ontario Trillium Foundation, the Ontario Heritage Trust, and the City of St. Thomas, along with many volunteer fundraisers. On the main floor, along with the Hall of Fame, the dining hall is once again a dining hall and event venue, while the second floor houses the offices of social services, lawyers, and politicians.

Lining the upper hallway are many of the more than eighty individuals, groups, structures, and culture tributes to Canada's railway heritage, inducted between 1999 and 2012. Among them is a singer-songwriter, Gordon Lightfoot, inducted for his iconic "Canadian Railroad Trilogy."

THE SHELTERS

Not all stations were grand. Many were built to fill a minimal role as simple shelters. Nevertheless, they reflect a now nearly forgotten role in Ontario's railway heritage. The tiny shelter that the Grand Trunk (GT) erected at Gilford near Lake Simcoe in 1890, on what had originally been the Ontario, Simcoe, and Huron Railway, is now restored in the Simcoe

County Museum. It displays four small, connected "dormers" at the peak of the pyramid roof. At least it had windows and a door. A much smaller, unadorned shelter is that from Sturgeon Bay on the Midland Railway, now displayed at the Canadian Heritage Museum in Coldwater. With no windows, this "out-house"-sized shelter was standing-room only.

The Moulinette GT shelter, rescued from the rising waters of the St. Lawrence Seaway, lies in the Lost Villages Historical Society Museum grounds near Long Sault.

The decorative wooden Toronto, Grey and Bruce shelter, built originally in 1882 at the country flag stop of Crombies, north of Orangeville,

St. Thomas' 1873 Canada Southern station is one of Ontario's oldest and largest stations. It was rescued from demolition by a concerted community campaign and now houses the North America Railway Hall of Fame.

has been rescued and now resides in the Dufferin County Museum on Airport Road at Highway 89. In the Franco-Ontarian town of Embrun, the Ottawa and New York Railway shelter, originally in Berwick, stands by a short rail trail and is now restored. The GT's attractive wooden Longwoods shelter has found a home at the Komoka Railway Museum.

On the grounds of the railway museum in Smiths Falls, an unusual shelter from Nolans originated as the base of a water tower.

Many other shelters rescued from demolition survive in various private backyards across the province.

All in all, Ontario can still boast of 140 railway stations, including those still in railway use and the many that have been rescued.

— 5 —
THE CASTLES OF THE LINE:
ONTARIO'S RAILWAY HOTELS

Many of Canada's grandest hotels were those built by the railway companies. Rail was, after all, the only way to travel comfortably, and travellers needed equally comfortable facilities at which to stay. In the smaller communities, such hostelries were often a quite simple inn, perhaps a couple of storeys in height, and seldom built by the railway companies. They would usually be found very close to the station itself. But, in the larger cities, with the major rail lines competing fiercely with one another, they hired architects to conceive grander hotels to attract more passengers.

Among the earliest of the grand railway hotels was the Banff Springs Hotel championed by the Canadian Pacific Railway's inveterate president, William Cornelius Van Horne. The Grand Trunk and the Canadian Northern Railways were hard on his heels, adding hotels like the Nova Scotian in Halifax, the Château Laurier in Ottawa, the Bessborough in Saskatoon (built actually by Canadian National), and the Fort Garry in Winnipeg.

THE ROYAL YORK, TORONTO

With the arrival of the railway lines along Toronto's Lake Ontario shoreline in 1853, the corner of Front Street and York, across the intersection from Toronto's first union station, was prime real estate for a hotel. The first to occupy the site was the Swords Hotel built in 1853, the same year that trains first began steaming into Toronto's simple, wooden

Union Station. In 1862, the Queens Hotel replaced it and was considered to be Toronto's finest.

That building would last for sixty-five years.

Following the death of the last owner, Henry Winnett, the property was sold to the Canadian Pacific Railway (CPR), one of the country's preeminent hotel builders.

The CPR's then-president, Sir William Beatty, commissioned the firm of Ross and MacDonald, designers of the Union Station that opened the same year, to design the hotel.

Opened in 1929, the Royal York Hotel would boast ten elevators, more than one thousand rooms, including the Royal Suite, and a telephone switchboard more than 30 metres long with more than five-dozen operators. The structure could also boast a hospital, library, and an enclosed rooftop garden. A row of twelve two-storey arched

The grand ballroom in the Fairmont Royal York Hotel is characteristic of the opulence of Canada's early railway hotels.

windows above the entrance mark the site of the ballroom, while a Château-style copper roof tops the tiered limestone structure.

A tunnel provided direct access to Union Station, directly across the road on Front Street. The hotel would reign for a full year as the British Empire's tallest building until it was overshadowed by the Bank of Commerce building in 1930.

Despite additions and renovations over the years, the hotel, now the Fairmont Royal York, retains the stunning grandeur that marked Canada's railway era. The two-storey foyer, with its clock, chandeliers, and double circular staircase, is a Toronto landmark in its own right. Wooden beams, marble pillars and floors, and metallic cornices create the atmosphere of opulence, which the Canadian Pacific Railway employed to mark its image.

The Imperial Room featured the big bands of Duke Ellington, Count Basie, and Woody Herman, singers like Tony Bennett, Eartha Kitt, and Pearl Bailey, and popular entertainers, namely the then-young comedian Jim Carrey and magician Doug Henning. When the format changed to Vegas-style shows, attendance declined. Following renovations in the 1990s it reopened as a banquet hall and event venue.

Among the more spectacular of the rooms are the third-floor ballroom, and the Canadian Room, which features wooden crests of the provinces and territories and a large carved wooden Canada crest as well. The Epic Restaurant in the lower level shows off the building's art deco designs, the style of choice when the hotel was built. The warm woodwork of the Library Bar and the comfortable chairs are another prominent feature of this historic place.

Out of sight, however, are the stairs leading to the roof where ghost hunters claim the ghost of a suicidal employee can be heard.

THE PRINCE ARTHUR HOTEL, THUNDER BAY

While it may lack the kind of grandeur that marks the Fairmont Royal York and the Fairmont Château Laurier, Thunder Bay's Prince Arthur Hotel does not lack for history.

According to the hotel's website, the birth of the hotel quite possibly took place in a private rail car belonging to Sir Donald Mann over a game of poker (although this has been questioned). In 1908, while en route to Winnipeg, Port Arthur's then-mayor John James Carrick was engaged in a friendly poker match with Mann and his co-creator of the Canadian Northern Railway, Sir William Mackenzie. As the evening wore on, facilitated no doubt by a few drams of brandy, Carrick began to lament that Port Arthur needed a railway hotel and that if Mackenzie and Mann were interested, he could come up with a piece of prime property directly across from where the Canadian Northern had built its grand new station.

The two agreed and in 1910 construction began. The following year, the hotel opened offering rooms with hot and cold running water. Guests at the opening feast dined on "caviar a la russo" and "essence of tomatoes en tasse." According to the hotel's press release of March 14, 1911, rooms on the first three floors were furnished in mahogany, the remainder in oak. The two-storey rotunda features murals and a dining room with a marble staircase entrance.

In 1920, the structure was enlarged to include a new dining room, a barber shop, and a newsstand, as well as a new wing.

The hotel's promotional literature unabashedly bragged that it was "one of the best-appointed hotels on the North American continent."

Unlike the châteauesque castles of Ottawa and Toronto, the Prince Arthur Hotel conveyed a much simpler plan, being square in shape, a mere four storeys, and topped with a flat roof.

The unusual tourist pagoda was part of the attempt to attract travellers to the Prince Arthur Hotel in what was then Port Arthur.

The tiered rear garden overlooked Lake Superior and the iconic rocky headland known as the Sleeping Giant. A sidewalk and stairs led to the twin-roofed Canadian Northern (CNo) station as well as the Canadian Pacific Railway (CPR) station. Tracks for the two rail lines paralleled each other and the stations were situated nearly opposite one another.

It was in this hotel in 1920 that the poppy allegedly became the symbol of remembrance for the First World War. Touched by the poem "In Flanders Fields" by Captain John McCrae, a French woman by the name of Anna Guérin began making poppies to raise funds for the war's widows and orphans, and travelled extensively to do so. One of her stops was at the Prince Arthur Hotel, where the local branch of the Great War Veterans Association (predecessor of the Canadian Legion) officially adopted the poppy as a symbol of remembrance. When other Canadian Legions followed suit, the poppy became the national symbol that it remains today.[1]

Much of the hotel is little-changed. The two-storey rotunda still greets guests who may enjoy a meal in the grand dining hall. The main entrance has shifted from the tracks to Cumberland Street, and most of what had been the garden has been turned over to parking. The CNo's tracks are gone, while those of the CPR remain. However, the latter's station came down to make way for a new roadway, while that of the former remains one of Thunder Bay's grandest buildings.

Part and parcel of the landscape around the hotel is the unusual pagoda. It was built across from the CNo and CPR stations in 1909 to serve as a tourist centre to welcome visitors arriving by rail or ship to an otherwise less-than-hospitable remote region. Built of brick, the octagonal building is topped by an Asian-influenced cupola. The roof bears the influence of a Hindu *chatri* roof, while Tuscan-style columns surround the main building. Bas-relief carvings of a beaver and maple leaves mark the entrance, while French doors and a Scandinavian dragon's head round out this multicultural edifice. Designed by local architect H. Russel Halton, and built by the port authority, the pagoda was declared a National Historic Site in 1988.

THE CHÂTEAU LAURIER, OTTAWA

This grand railway hotel is almost as iconic a symbol of Ottawa as are the Parliament Buildings. Indeed, because so many parliamentarians spent so much of their time there, it became known as the "third chamber."

Like much ado about Ottawa, the hotel's origins began in controversy. By the late 1890s, politicians and citizens alike were clamouring for a grand new hotel for the nation's capital. At that time, the president of the Grand Trunk was Charles Melville Hays, who shared the wish for a grand hotel. But the location remained contentious. The first proposal was for a ten-storey structure nearly opposite the Parliament Buildings, but this was firmly rejected as it would block the site lines to the buildings. Another location at Nepean Point was considered too far from downtown.

Eventually, the Liberal prime minister, Sir Wilfrid Laurier, offered a portion of Major's Hill Park, a popular open space at Wellington and Rideau Streets. In return, a grateful Hays would name it the Château Laurier, after the prime minister. Located beside the canal and central to both the downtown and parliament, it proved ideal, but again, not without opposition.

Hays hired the Montreal architectural firm of Ross and MacFarlane to design a 16th-century French château, this after the original architect Bradford Lee Gilbert was fired, again provoking much controversy. The new firm was to design not only the hotel but the proposed new union station across the road from it, connecting the two with a tunnel.

The building was finished by 1912 and a grand opening, along with that for the station, was planned for April 26, 1912, just as soon as Hays and his family returned from England on the *Titanic*. Hays did not survive that fateful sinking (his wife and daughter did survive) and the opening was postponed.

The new hotel featured Indiana limestone on a granite base, oak panelling in the lobby, and stained glass windows above the porticoed entrance. The lobby was designed to resemble an English hunting lodge and for a time was festooned with deer heads. In addition to its 350 rooms, the steep-roofed château offered private dining rooms, meeting rooms, and a corridor known as "Peacock Alley," modelled after the Peacock Alley in England's Windsor Castle.

In 1929, the hotel doubled in size with the addition of an east wing and an art deco swimming pool.

The grand hotel has been the choice of many of this nation's more famous people and events. In 1936, the Canadian Broadcasting Corporation launched its radio network from the seventh and eighth floors. Renowned portrait photographer Yousuf Karsh established his studios in the hotel's sixth floor, where between 1973 and 1992 he turned out his portraits, while he and his wife occupied Suite 358, now named in his honour. Fifteen of his portraits still hang in the hotel. Another famous resident was the late prime minister, R.H. Pierre Trudeau.

Despite a number of enlargements and renovations, this railway hotel, now the Fairmont Château Laurier, retains its heritage. The foyer still offers its bust of Laurier, and Peacock Alley remains one of the nation's grandest corridors, lined with heritage images. The art deco swimming pool, one of the few left, has been little altered, and even retains its original lamps. While the tunnel no longer brings rail travellers from the old station, which is now an out-of-bounds convention centre, it does open during conventions and Doors Open events. The room known today as "Zoe's Lounge" was the original concert hall, but perhaps the grandest room of all is the magnificent ballroom with its elaborate ceiling, and where glass doors on the second level provide private access.[2]

The Fairmont Château Laurier was conceived by GT president Charles Hays, but he never lived to enjoy its opening, having met his fate on the Titanic.

CPR'S FRENCH RIVER BUNGALOW CAMP

Canada's rail lines did not just offer luxury accommodation in the larger cities. They lured the rich and famous to resort areas as well. The Canadian Pacific Railway's Banff Springs Hotel and Château Lake Louise, the Château Montebello in Quebec,

and St. Andrews by the Sea in New Brunswick are all grand examples of what that line could offer. In return, the Canadian Northern and the Grand Trunk, later the Canadian National Railway, came back with their own Jasper Lodge, the Maniki Lodge (since burned), and the Highland Inn in Algonquin Park (demolished).

To add more rustic appeal, the Canadian Pacific Railway (CPR) also built a series of what it called "bungalow camps." Two in Ontario included the Devils Gap on Lake of the Woods, and the French River Bungalow Camp on Ontario's scenic and historic French River.

In 1912, the CPR had completed what would become its main line between Toronto and Sudbury. Sixty kilometres south of Sudbury the track crossed the fabled French River on a truss bridge. On the north side of the river, a high rocky promontory offered magnificent views down the channel of the river, while its waters boasted abundant fishing.

And so it was here that in 1923 the CPR built a resort-style station and added what they called their French River Bungalow Camp. Along the cliff were a string of bungalows, or cabins, and a high wooden water tower, beneath which stood the main lodge with log walls and a stone fireplace.

Not only did the peaceful location attract many wealthy Americans, but royalty as well. In 1939, on their cross-country tour to encourage the purchase of war bonds, King George VI and the then-Queen Elizabeth, the mother of the current monarch, dined in the lodge. In tribute, the CPR incorporated a rough version of the royal crown into the fireplace, although their majesties opted to sleep in their private coach.

The stone fireplace in the CPR's French River Bungalow Camp incorporated a version of the royal crown to commemorate a visit by King George VI and the then-Queen Elizabeth.

Visiting members of Hollywood "royalty" included Clarke Gable, Ray Bolger, and Marilyn Monroe. Perhaps the appeal was to distance themselves from the press and the public pressures of Tinsel Town. Monroe usually chose Cabin 15, where the apparition of a lovely blond woman is said to occasionally appear.[3]

The camp still stands, known in recent times as Yesterday's Resort and Conference Centre. The cabins still overlook the cliff-lined French River channel and the main lodge still has the "royal" fireplace. Even the aging wooden water tower still looms high above the resort. The CPR station was moved across the tracks and now serves as a private residence.

Meanwhile, portions of the Devil's Gap resort survive on the Lake of the Woods, but its ownership is the subject of a dispute.

THE EMPIRE HOTEL, NORTH BAY

While the Empire Hotel in North Bay was not built by any of the major railways, its construction and location were influenced by the city's importance as a railway hub. The hotel was designed and built by Leo Mascioli and V. Bardessono. Begun in 1927, it opened within a year. The Canadian Northern Railway station (by then co-shared between the Canadian National, Temiskaming, and Northern Ontario Railways) lay a few blocks north on Fraser Street, while the elegant stone station erected by the Canadian Pacific Railway rested a short distance east on Oak Street, both within walking distance.

When the hotel opened in 1928, the North Bay *Nugget* newspaper noted that of the thirty-five airy rooms on each floor, twenty-five contained a bath, and ten offered hot and cold running water. The Howard Johnson chain operated the hotel during the last quarter of the twentieth century. Then, in 2004, it was renovated to become a retirement living centre and more than doubled in size.

Fortunately, many heritage features remain, including decorative columns and cornices. The main dining room retains such original heritage components as columns, pilasters, beams, and ceiling moldings. But perhaps the most interesting of all is the grand ballroom where, as the City of North Bay heritage report notes: "The ceilings are an excellent example of craftsmanship imported from Italy…. The coffers are a deeply recessed octagon surrounded with a floral and scroll work motif…. Lined with egg and dart moldings, and a double floral medallion … the beams supporting the ceiling have an intricate series of dentals, egg and dart, surface reliefs and columns."

The exterior, by contrast, was a simple five-storey, flat-roof structure, which belies the more elaborate interior. The building, however, is not open to the public, except during the occasional "Doors Open" event.

Other hotels influenced by the railways included the Kenricia in Kenora, the "Ceeps" in London, and others in many smaller towns and villages across Ontario.

LIFE ON THE LINE:

HOW RAILWAY MEN (AND WOMEN) LIVED

Among the often forgotten components of Ontario's railway heritage were the many forms of railway accommodation. These ranged from the crew's bunkhouses, the station masters' homes, workers' housing, and to the grand mansions of the railway builders themselves. And then there were the forgotten Railway YMCAs.

THE BUILDERS

YATES CASTLE, BRANTFORD

This fanciful Tudoresque mansion showed how the builders of the railways lived. Henry Yates made many millions promoting the Great Western Railway. In 1864, he constructed a mighty mansion overlooking the Buffalo and Lake Huron rail line which passed through Brantford mere metres from the building. Naming his castle "Wynarden," he added a fenced garden with stone entrance, a carriage house, a brick cellar accessed through a trap door, separate servants' quarters, and a private school. The property also boasted a fountain and four greenhouses.

Inside he added a wine cellar, a billiards room, stained glass windows, and lavatories with hot and cold running water. The exterior is a mix of towers, turrets, high gables, and elaborate fretwork which also featured embossed crests, emblems, and a seven-sided chimney. In recent times the interior was renovated to accommodate eight separate apartments. While a small railway community gradually grew around it, the castle still looms above the busy CN rail yards.

MACKENZIE HOUSE, KIRKFIELD

One of Canada's pre-eminent railway builders, William Mackenzie, was born in 1846 near the community of Kirkfield, Ontario, then little more than a stage stop on a busy pioneer road. But Mackenzie soon became involved with his main love, the railways. Along with partner Donald Mann, the two cobbled together a nation-wide rail network from uneconomical branch lines and unused railway charters, creating the Canadian Northern Railway (CNo). After being knighted in 1911, he expanded his interests into electrical power and electrically run rail lines. The CNo was still expanding in 1918, when with funds going to the war effort, financing dried up and the line plunged into bankruptcy.

With his many early railway contracts, including one with the Canadian Pacific Railway in the prairies, Mackenzie was able to build a grand home on the outskirts of Kirkfield. The main entrance hall featured a large fireplace and panelled walls. The dining room boasted French tapestries, while the drawing and music rooms were hung with Louis XVI damask, where white woodwork was flecked with gold. Wealthy associates from Toronto would travel there on what began as the Nipissing Railway.

But in the 1920s, Mackenzie's international clout was waning and he died in 1923. He lies buried nearby. The handsome wood mansion has since passed through a variety of owners and uses, including that of a bed and breakfast.

DONALD MANN'S FALLINGBROOK, TORONTO

In 1907, Mackenzie's partner Donald Mann built a fine home of his own. Located on a bluff overlooking Lake Ontario he named his mansion "Fallingbrook." The building stood two and a half storeys in height and featured a half-timbered second storey with wide hip-gable dormers above a stone ground floor. Inside were Chippendale chairs, Dutch tapestry, valuable rare oil paintings, and silk drapes and hangings. A miniature version of this castle was built on Kingston Road and served as the grounds' gatehouse. Sadly, on January 27, 1930, Fallingbrook was lost to flames. The small half-timbered gatehouse still stands on Kingston Road, now out of place among the post-war bungalows. "Fallingbrook" survives only in the street name, which now links Kingston Road with the east end of Queen Street.

BOOTH'S MANSION, OTTAWA

John Rudolphus Booth was, in his day, the continent's wealthiest railway man. From a poor farm in rural Quebec, he moved to Ottawa where he established some of that city's most extensive sawmill operations. His bounty began when he was awarded the contract to supply the lumber for Canada's first parliament buildings and surged when he acquired the vast timber limits in Algonquin Park for a sum of $15,000.

To access this timber, he built a railway to move the logs. Known as the Ottawa, Arnprior and Parry Sound Railway, it was part of his larger Canada Atlantic Railway network. He laid tracks from Ottawa not just through the park, but to the shores of Georgian Bay where he bypassed the expectant town of Parry Sound and created a new town on the shores of Parry Island, a town he called Depot Harbour.

Following the fires that ravaged his mills and consumed much of Ottawa in 1904, Mann sold the railway to the Grand Trunk for $1.4 million.

He used his wealth to erect a grand stone mansion which was destroyed in the earlier devastating fire of 1900. In 1909 he replaced it with a large brick mansion on Metcalfe Street, featuring hand-carved wood, Italian marble floors, and eight fireplaces. Designed by John W.H. Watts in the "Queen Anne" style, the exterior boasted multiple projections, elaborate decorative gables, and a castellated square corner tower.

Following Booth's death in 1925, at age ninety-nine, the mansion remained in the family until 1947 when the Laurentian Club of Ottawa purchased the home, making only modest changes. The federal government in 1990 designated the mansion as a national historic site. In 2001, Trinity Western University bought the building for a leadership centre and student residence. A strong earthquake in 2010 damaged two chimneys and a wall, the repairs for which were split between the university and the federal government. The building stands at 252 Metcalfe Street.

ALAN MACNAB'S DUNDURN CASTLE, HAMILTON

Alan Napier MacNab, later knighted, had built his Dundurn Castle well before he entered the business of building and promoting railways. From being an 1812 war hero he became an active politician, partaking in the railway business in 1845 when he became the president of the nascent Great Western Railway (GW), a position he held from 1845 to 1854. When the GW line reached Hamilton in 1853, the yards were laid coincidentally beneath the high bluffs upon which he had built Dundurn Castle.

The building had been finished two decades earlier in 1835 at a cost of $175,000. It featured gas lights, running water, and a "dumb waiter" elevator system, as well as seventy-two rooms. From 1854 to 1860 MacNab served on the boards of at least a half dozen other railways and once proclaimed "all my politics are railroads."

Gradually MacNab sank deeper into debt and, following his death in 1862, his estate had to sell the castle to pay off his debts. The building is now a popular museum, while his rail yard far below still throbs with the engines of diesel locomotives.

FRANCIS CLERGUE'S MONTFERMIER, SAULT STE. MARIE

This feisty entrepreneur arrived in Sault Ste. Marie in 1894 and began the industrial empire that would become Algoma Steel and the Algoma Central Railway. In 1903, the empire appeared to be on the verge of collapse only to be resuscitated a year later. Still, he found enough money to build a mansion overlooking his empire. Naming it "Montfermier," he situated it on the brow of Moffley Hill. Like many of the Sault Ste. Marie's grand buildings, he used the warm, local red sandstone for the exterior. A circular mahogany staircase led to the six bedrooms on the second floor, while also overlooking the view on the ground floor of the grand dining room, capable of seating up to sixty dinner guests. By 1909, the Clergues had left Sault Ste. Marie, and the mansion passed through various owners until it was destroyed by fire in 1934. Today, nothing remains of the mansion of this empire-builder.

GEORGE GOODERHAM'S WAVENEY, TORONTO

The name Gooderham has left many a legacy landmark on the city of Toronto. The name is most familiarly linked with the iconic Gooderham and Worts Distillery, which operated from its beginnings as a wind-powered grist mill on the west bank of the Don River in 1837 until its ultimate closure in 1990. The later buildings of that industrial complex remain almost totally intact, now a popular attraction known as the Distillery District.

But besides the distillery, the Gooderhams were heavily involved in building some of Ontario's vital railway lines, in particular the Toronto, Grey and Bruce and the Toronto and Nipissing Railways, whose station stood beside the vast complex. Much of the rationale for distilleries getting into railways was to ensure a reliable means of shipping raw materials to the factories.

Another iconic Gooderham landmark is the elegant pie-shaped flat-iron building situated at Wellington and Front Street. His mansion, a Romanesque red brick-and-stone hulk, which Gooderham named Waveney after a river in England, dominates the corner of Bloor Street West and St. George Street, in what was then the up-and-coming Annex, home of the city's nouveau riche. Gooderham died in 1905, worth more than $25 million, and in 1910 the mansion passed into the hands of the York Club. The interior remains little altered, while the exterior boasts grand towers and gables.

EDWARD WALKER'S WILLISTEAD, WALKERVILLE

Another of Ontario's leading booze kings and railway builders was Hiram Walker. In the late 1850s he began to distill whisky at a location on the Detroit River, just east of Windsor. Here he laid out the town of Walkerville and established a rail line to access the raw material needed for the operation, the Lake Erie and Detroit River Railway (LEDR).

Those tracks are gone now, as are most of the stations along it, save the Richardsonian Romanesque stone stations at Kingsville and Essex. But it was his son, Edward, who in 1906 hired renowned architect Albert Kahn to design the Walker mansion, known as "Willistead." Here, on 16 acres of land at the south end of Walkerville, arose a grand country manor with half-timbered walls and gables, a 14-metre (42-foot) great hall with oak panelling, and a wide stairway with carved railings. The dining room featured mahogany wainscotting, a massive brass chandelier, and a fireplace with Italian marble. Among the many rooms were a billiards room, a ladies' parlour, and a library. Now owned by the City of Windsor, which has made a number of alterations, the building is open on occasion to the public.

The early LEDR Walkerville station has been gone for a more than a decade, although VIA Rails' modernistic Walkerville station, the line, a legacy of the Grand Trunk, still welcomes several daily trains from Toronto.[1]

THE RAILWAY WORKERS

RAILWAY YMCAS

While the kings of the line lived in grand style, the ordinary linemen, engineers, brakemen, and maintenance-of-way staff all had to endure simpler, if not outright brutal, living conditions.

Often their home away from home would be little more than a converted boxcar.

Although the link between railways and the YMCA movement dates back to 1844 in London, England, Ontario's first Railway "Y" appeared in St. Thomas in 1881. In 1896, Charles M. Hays, then president of the Grand Trunk, urged D.A. Budge, secretary general of the YMCA, to visit the Grand Trunk's divisional points. In 1906, Budge went on to visit those of the Canadian Pacific Railway as well. So appalling did he find the conditions that he immediately initiated a program to establish YMCA facilities at as many of these locations as were needed.

While many of the early Ys were housed in converted buildings, the first purpose-built Y was that built for the Canadian Northern Railway near the rail yards at the foot of Spadina Avenue in Toronto. Within twenty years, twenty-eight Railway YMCA's had been established, many of them in Ontario. In the north where conditions were most severe, Ys appeared in Kenora, Sioux Lookout, Schreiber, Chapleau, Cartier, Ignace, Hornepayne, and White River, while in the south communities like Allandale, Sarnia, Stratford, St. Thomas, Fort Erie, and Niagara Falls could claim Railway Ys. Toronto alone had four.[2]

With dieselization, fewer divisional points were needed. The railways began to add new bunkhouses and in the 1950s the Railway YMCA department was disbanded. Those buildings that weren't demolished became community Ys and even these are gone, the last to go in Sioux Lookout in 1994. Only one former Railway Y still stands, that at Allandale, now a popular bar and grill in Barrie, known today as Beaches Fine Market Grill. The attractive red brick structure is three stories in height and sports a corner tower with a mansard roof.

WORKERS' HOUSING

Across northern Ontario, the railway towns rose from scratch. Unlike the south where the rail lines encountered existing towns and villages, and where accommodation could be found, the railways had to build their own housing for the train crews. While overnight facilities, either in bunkhouses or Railway Ys, were available at the turnaround points,

The only surviving former Railway YMCA building is now a popular bar and grill located behind the Allandale train station in Barrie.

home terminals required permanent houses. Here too the railway lines dipped into their pattern books to create rows of standard looking homes.

Most were two-storey duplexes, although other single dwellings might have a more distinctive roofline (examples of these yet stand in White River). In White River, the Canadian Pacific Railway actually played the role of municipal council until a municipality was incorporated. Gradually the railways sold the buildings to their employees and even to ordinary buyers. In many communities, the lookalike rows of houses were modernized or replaced entirely.

Examples of standard employee housing are yet evident in place like Schreiber, Cartier, Nakina, White River, Chapleau, and MacTier.

Early railway bunkhouses were also of a standard concept, usually two stories in height. Most are gone now, having been replaced in the 1960s and 1970s with newer facilities, or demolished entirely. The oldest of Ontario's in-use railway bunkhouses is that in White River, built in 1948. Newer such facilities were later added in places like Brent, Hornepayne, and Rainy River. Others appeared in Fort Erie and South Parry. With the reduction in rail traffic, many of these have been removed. A small

Typical railway housing lines a residential street in Schreiber.

motel-like range of rooms remains in use by CN employees at Hawk Junction, as does a residence in Rainy River. An experiment in Hornepayne, known as the Hallmark Centre, opened in 1980 and incorporated into one complex, a hotel, a senior's residence, a liquor store, library, swimming pool, and CN employee housing. Unfortunately in 2010 the lease expired and the tenants evicted. The building remained vacant in 2012.

Despite being isolated, railway employees throughout northern Ontario interacted with each other along the line. Baseball and hockey teams competed with each other, a few even initiated arts groups including theatrical and musical groups. The expansion of northern Ontario's highway network in the 1960s meant such groups no longer depended upon the railways and became community groups relying upon cars rather than coaches.

The railway museum in Stirling's former train station depicts typical station accommodation for the agent and his family.

At least these employees enjoyed life in a community where they engaged in sports, orchestras, and social clubs. The section foremen and their families were less fortunate — they lived in isolated houses situated at intervals along the remote lines. Occasionally they would have visits from travelling dentists and school cars, but little else. Finally, the expansion of northern Ontario's highway network in the 1960s removed the isolation, and section crews moved to more centralized locations that were highway accessible. Where such structures still remain, they have become cabins or hunt camps, or, as in the case of the Algoma Central Railway, stations to serve the remote recreational facilities along the line.

For the railway station agents, the station itself was often their home. While some form of housing could usually be found in the larger towns and villages, it was in the more remote locations that the agents lived in their stations. That is why many rural stations contained an upper floor, where the agent and his family enjoyed their bedrooms. Kitchen and dining room were often on the ground floor at the rear of the building. A separate dwelling for the station agent was built by the Temiskaming and Northern Ontario (T&NO) in Latchford and still stands. Major rail lines like the Great Western, the Grand Trunk, the T&NO, and the Canadian Pacific Railway all devised station patterns which could be repeated all along the line and which featured accommodation for the agent and his family.

The best example of a rural station that has preserved these features is the Stirling Grand Trunk Railway Station museum. Otherwise, there are no remaining examples of active station agents who continue to live in a station.

— 7 —

FORGOTTEN STRUCTURES:

OF ROUNDHOUSES, WATER TOWERS, AND COAL CHUTES

Railway features like bridges and stations continue to stand out on the landscape. While some remain in railway use, others survive, now reused. Former stations may house community centres, restaurants, museums, or craft shops. Abandoned bridges frequently form a portion of various rail trails where hikers, cyclists, or ATV riders follow the paths of the railway engineers.

But today's generation of rail travellers or trail users would likely be unaware of the great variety of other structures upon which the railways depended to keep the trains running.

THE ROUNDHOUSES[1]

Perhaps besides the stations, the most prominent structures were the railway roundhouses. In the days of steam every divisional point had one. It was here that the steam engines puffed onto a turntable which would swing the mighty machine towards an empty stall into which the engine would creep for maintenance and repair. They were called "round" houses because of their semi-circular configuration around the turntable.

This type of railway building evolved in Europe, as engines needed repairing away from the elements. In the 1820s, the earliest versions were simple square shelters with the tracks running through them. Engines came in one end and out the other. A second version had the engines coming in and out the same entrance. But finally, the roundhouse reigned supreme: with its turntable in front it saved space and was easier to enlarge. The term "stalls" for the engines originates from the days of horse-drawn transport. These buildings would often include machine shops and crew quarters. The first known roundhouse was that in Camden, England in 1840.

Ontario's first engine house was likely that built in 1853 by the Great Western Railway at its Hamilton headquarters, followed ten years later by Ontario's first known roundhouse at this site. By 1859, the Grand Trunk was on the scene, and was reported to have erected engine houses at Brockville, Kingston, Toronto, and London. Many of these were in fact cross-shaped with a turntable in the middle.

The Chapleau turntable still directs the CPR locomotives into their engine house stalls.

As roundhouses replaced the engine house, different railways employed distinctive door designs, such as that in Owen Sound, where in 1883 the Toronto, Grey and Bruce (CPR) used arched transoms above the doors. Then, as rail lines upgraded their networks, roundhouse styles became more standard.

To accommodate the growing size of the steam locomotives, the rail lines enlarged the stalls to 28 metres (80 feet) and added smoke jacks above them to ventilate the smoke. Other improvements included fireproofing, which began in 1901, and reinforced concrete in 1905. Before entering the turntable, and then the stall, the roundhouse workers would empty the engine's ashes, and then move the engine to the coal chute, and finally the water tower.

By 1950, Ontario could claim more than sixty roundhouses, many of which survived into the 1990s, servicing diesels. Those in Toronto alone numbered nearly a dozen. But with no viable re-use potential, namely because of their remote locations within the yards and the more modern servicing facilities available, nearly all have been removed. Local efforts to save them in places like Belleville and the Lambton yard in west-end Toronto, fell upon deaf ears. Today only one actual roundhouse remains in railway use, that at Sault Ste. Marie, while an early engine house in Chapleau still employs a turntable.

The Ottawa, Arnprior and Parry Sound Railway (also known as the Booth Line) constructed roundhouses in Madawaska and Depot Harbour in the 1890s. These were later replaced by the Grand Trunk and the Canadian National Railways. When the line was abandoned, both lay in ruin. That in Madawaska was demolished in the 1990s, while that in Depot Harbour still rises like a Roman ruin above a young forest. Bannockburn represented the terminus of the Bay of Quinte Railway and here remains the shell of the two-stall engine house. It lies, however, on private property.

Modern facilities continue to function in the larger rail yards, as even the most modern diesel locomotives require regular maintenance, but few of these buildings would qualify as a "heritage" structure.

OTHER FORGOTTEN STRUCTURES

Most divisional points also had coal chutes. These large towers of wood or concrete would contain vast amounts of coal, which would thunder down into the coal tenders to feed the fires of the locomotives. While nearly all of those that were constructed of wood were removed, a number of the concrete coal chutes, being more costly to demolish, may yet be seen looming above the rights-of-way, usually at some distance from the stations. These may yet be seen in Toronto at the Roundhouse Park, Washago, South River, Hornepayne, and Foleyet

Great quantities of water, fired by the coal, boiled into the great gushes of steam that drove the pistons of the locomotives. Because water was consumed quickly, water towers were a sight at alternate stations along the lines. A long gauge, which rested on a float and protruded through the top of the tank, indicated the level of the water that remained in the tank. To avoid freezing, pumps at the base of the tower would circulate the water in the tank. While most were constructed of wood above a concrete or stone base, many were also made of steel.

The end of steam doomed most of these gangly towers and today only a small handful remains. None, however, remain in use. Those in Pembroke, Barry's Bay, and Blyth have survived intact, while

Elgin County Railway Museum volunteer, Daniel, demonstrates the use of levers in the Museum's BX interlocking tower in St. Thomas.

a trio of water towers lines the Canadian Pacific Railway (CPR) tracks in eastern Ontario — two in Monckland and Chesterville, respectively, and a third a few metres over the Quebec border in Dalhousie Station. The latter, with its wooden tank above a stone base, has clearly been privately restored, while the former, likely identical to that in Dalhousie Mills originally, now contain a cement tank above the stone base. Both serve as storage for the CPR.

Railway divisional points, junctions, and crossings were often a jumble of interconnecting rails. As trains arrived and departed, some semblance of order was essential, and this was the responsibility of the switching tower. These were typically two storeys in height to allow the switcher to keep watch over the train movements. A row of levers connected by long steel rods to the switches would allow him to manoeuvre the oncoming trains onto the correct tracks. But as longer unit trains began to replace the local trains, less switching was needed, and those manoeuvres that were required were often controlled from distant computer-operated, centralized control operations. And so, with little potential for adaptive re-use, most were demolished.

A similar structure, the crossing towers where watchmen guarded road crossings, have long vanished from the landscape with the construction of grade separations and improved crossing signals.

SURVIVING STRUCTURES

ALLANDALE (BARRIE)

Once a separate community from Barrie, Allandale was one of southern Ontario's most important rail hubs. When the mighty and expanding Grand Trunk Railway (GT) absorbed the many small lines that converged here, the line established a major yard operation. Here, in 1905, the GT built one of the province's most elegant wooden stations. Now restored wonderfully by the City of Barrie, the station, as of late 2012, was awaiting a tenant.

Beside the building that formerly served as the Railway YMCA (Ontario's last), the vacant freight shed yet stands, occupied by a private business.

The busy tracks that once carried freight and passenger trains by the Lake Simcoe side of the station now carries four lanes of cars. But, still on its original site overlooking the lake, is the Canadian National Railway's one-time master mechanic's building. Preserved outside and in, it now serves as a tourist office and, in an addition to the building, an event venue. Nearby, although the turntable pit has been filled in more recently, the cement pads of the twenty-seven-stall roundhouse lie overgrown by the parking lot. An attractive waterside park carries strollers and cyclists along the water's edge.

Rail activity has returned with the opening, in 2012, of a much-needed and overdue GO station.

BARRY'S BAY

Until the 1890s, the little logging outpost of Barry's Bay, situated on the north end of Kamaniskeg Lake, was little more than a clutch of log shacks around a steamer landing. Then, in the 1890s, lumber tycoon John Rudolphus Booth began laying out a legendary railway line that would link his extensive

In Barry's Bay, the historic railway water tower is preserved near the town's heritage station.

sawmill operation in Ottawa with his timber limits in Algonquin Park, and eventually to Georgian Bay, where on the shores of Parry Island he would lay out the townsite of Depot Harbour.

With its steamer connections and important supply of water, Booth located in Barry's Bay one of his standard-plan stations and a nearby water tower. Barry's Bay has evolved in recent years to become a bustling regional centre and tourist town. Part of the attraction is the station, which has become a museum, but also the original water tower, Ontario's only surviving wooden water tower. It remains intact and protected from vandals by a fence. The Tuscan red tower, with its float rod yet penetrating its roof, looks out of place now that tracks have given way to roads and new housing.

BLYTH

These days the bustling town of Blyth in southwestern Ontario is better known for its theatre than for its railway heritage. But the latter survives. The town boomed with the arrival of the Guelph and Goderich Railway in 1908, a line operated by the Canadian Pacific Railway. Here, the railway constructed one of its standard stations and added a water tower as well. Being one of the newer water towers, this one was built of steel rather than wood. Although it fell out of use when diesel locomotives replaced those run by steam, the tower remains beside what is now a rail trail. The station itself stands a short distance away, well-preserved and part of a retail operation. Still in situ is the diminutive brick "witch's hat" station on the London, Huron, and Bruce Railway, now functioning as a bed and breakfast.

CARLETON PLACE

Ontario's oldest surviving roundhouse is that in Carleton Place. It was erected by the Canadian Pacific Railway (CPR) in 1887 and, like many of that line's Ottawa Valley structures, was constructed of stone. Built by Pembroke contractor J.W. Monroe, its fifteen stalls were 15 metres (75 feet) in length and the doors were 5 metres (16 feet) high.

The building, along with the attached car shop, was acquired by the Canada Wool Growers Association in 1942. Although much of the roundhouse has been altered, the car shop yet displays its high ceiling and even a few tracks. A date stone inscribed with "AD 1887" marks the door to the car shop, where various railway photos and artifacts can be seen in a small display area.

But that's not all. A few short blocks away, the CPR station also survives, having been the railway's sole Ottawa Valley stone station to avoid its company's busy wrecking balls, and has a variety of tenants.

The stone engine house in Carleton Place is now preserved by the Canadian Wool Growers Association.

CAPREOL

Still a busy divisional point, the yards at Capreol have retained the remains of its early roundhouse. Its first roundhouse lay on the west side of the Vermilion River and was built in 1906 by the Canadian Northern Railway (CNo). In 1914, the CNo moved its tracks to the east side and established an extensive rail yard with a large two-storey station, in addition to a larger roundhouse. This is where the CNo's tracks from Ottawa and Toronto merged to form the line's route to the west. The station was replaced in the 1990s, and a once-popular Railway YMCA no longer stands. The roundhouse at the north end of the yards now houses an industrial tenant, and although the turntable pit was filled in, its location can still be discerned.

CHAPLEAU

Now a popular jumping-off point for fishers and hunters, Chapleau remains all railway. Here, the vast yards yet throb with heavy diesel locomotives, while hard-hatted train crews change their shifts. Even VIA Rail's local Sudbury to White River train, the *Superior*, still stops here. Although the current station is modern, the freight station dates from the 1920s, while across the yards a turntable still guides the large diesels into one of the four bays in the historic engine house, the oldest structure in the yard. Although square rather than semi-circular, the structure fills the same role as a roundhouse.

HORNEPAYNE

Inveterate railway builders William Mackenzie and Donald Mann decided to establish a major divisional point at Hornepayne. In 1915, they laid out extensive yards, and erected a large two-storey station and a roundhouse. After the Canadian National Railway (CNR) assumed the bankrupt Canadian Northern (CNo) assets, it replaced the station and then built one of the north's distinctive oddities: a "square" roundhouse. It was built in 1921 by the CNR to replace the CNo's earlier fourteen-stall, more traditional roundhouse.

The turntable was built 28 metres (80 feet) long to accommodate the longer steam locomotives of that era. The concrete foundation extends more than 2 metres below-grade to mitigate the cold. Designed by architect G.C. Briggs, it measures 78 metres (288 feet) by 70 metres (223 feet) and covers 7,500 square metres (64,000 square feet). Because of the bitter winter temperatures, the turntable and stalls needed to be housed inside the facility rather than outside. While the structure is no longer an active roundhouse, it remains in good repair.

Nevertheless, the community, like Chapleau, is all railway, employing 200–250 CNR and VIA workers, all housed in new facilities along with a small VIA waiting room, for here the mighty VIA *Canadian* pauses for 20–25 minutes to allow a crew change, and for passengers to stretch their legs and take in the sights of a genuine railway town.

Longo's Supermarket has moved into the CNo locomotive shop in Leaside, saving the historic building.

LEASIDE

Despite the Canadian Pacific Railway (CPR) having built Leaside's first station, it was the Canadian Northern Railway (CNo) of Mackenzie and Mann that created Leaside's main railway presence. In 1908, they began work on their Toronto to Parry Sound route, which was to be a major link in their cross-country railway route to the Pacific. Making their way up the Don River Valley, they first established a yard beneath where the Bloor viaduct today stands. But limited space and flooding forced them elsewhere, and that would be the open table land above the valley.

But this meant building a branch from their main tracks, which emerged from the valley, some distance to the north. After creating this stub line via running rights on the CPR, they went about laying out a townsite that they named Leaside, though it remained largely undeveloped for another two decades. Here too they laid out yards and built a large number of railway structures including a roundhouse, yard station, passenger car shop, and a large brick locomotive shop. A transfer table was situated between the coach shop and the locomotive shop. The locomotive shop opened in 1919 and was built to a standard plan devised by the CNo in 1906.[2]

By the 1920s, the Canadian National Railway (CNR) had taken over the bankrupt CNo, moving most of the facilities to Stratford, but continued to operate the yard until the 1970s. Over the ensuing years, the remaining operations ended and tracks were removed. However, the locomotive shop, which passed through a variety of industrial owners, in 2008 earned a heritage designation that prevented its demolition. Today, its appearance both outside and in retains key architectural features. On the ground floor however, the tracks and the machinery for servicing the locomotives have been replaced by zucchinis, sausages, and cereal boxes, as the historic shops are now the home of one of Toronto's largest and newest Longo's supermarkets.

London

In London, a much older roundhouse dating to the days of the Great Western Railway has been altered to house the Great West Beef Company restaurant.

Despite additions, many of its features remain visible both outside and in. Constructed of brick around 1860, the arched stall entrances remain visible and include a 1860s-era Great Western steam locomotive display. As of 2012, this roundhouse was for sale.

SAULT STE. MARIE.

Like that in Hornepayne, the Algoma Central Railway (ACR) roundhouse in Sault Ste. Marie is square, but this one is still in use. Built in 1912, and larger than that in Hornepayne, it covers more than 9,000 square metres (72,000 square feet) and was designed by P.L. Bottey of the Arnold Company of Chicago. At one end of the sprawling brick structure, the wide turntable still survives, while at the other end coaches and freight cars await maintenance and repair. The vast and bustling yards at the "Soo" also contain other historic structures such as a machine shop and former coach shop.

ST. THOMAS

St. Thomas bills itself as "Railway City," and for good reason. First, it has undertaken one of Ontario's most outstanding railway station preservations, converting one of the province's longest brick stations, long vacant, into a railway hall of fame, event venue, and offices. Across the former yard, the Elgin County Railway Museum houses one of the province's most extensive collections of railway rolling stock in what was once the Michigan Central Railway's car shops.

A pair of roundhouses and a car shop occupied the grounds nearby, but have now been removed. The 6,000-square-metre shops were built in 1913 and continue to function as the museum's locomotive repair facility, the oldest in North America to continuously do so.

A short distance west of the yards, the museum has also preserved the "BX" interlocking tower. It was built in 1910 at what was then the intersection of the Michigan Central and the London and Port Stanley railways. Atop the two-storey flight of exterior stairs, the brick cabin houses forty levers — twenty for signals and twenty for actual switching. A mechanical interlocking grid serves to prevent the operator-leverman from inadvertently switching trains onto tracks with other active traffic. During the heyday of rail movements, more than one hundred switching operations would happen each shift. Early communications equipment is also on display, and the tower is open for viewing during special museum event days.

The unusual indoor roundhouse in Sault Ste. Marie is still used by CN Rail.

SARNIA

Here at the far southwest section of Sarnia's vast CN Rail yards, a roundhouse clings to life. Built by the CN shortly after it had assumed the assets of the Grand Trunk, the brick structure still consists of four stalls, although the turntable pit is now filled in. The roundhouse now contains private industrial tenants.

STRATFORD

Another of Ontario's major rail facilities was that at Stratford. Located on a source of water in the midst of southwestern Ontario, Stratford grew from a Grand Trunk (GT) railway junction in 1856 into one the Canadian National Railway's largest rail hubs.

The Grand Trunk (GT) arrived in Stratford in 1856 where the Buffalo and Lake Huron Railway had already built its own shops. When the GT bought out the older line in 1865, it took over the shops, and within five years was building shops of its own.

Following the GT's takeover of the Great Western (GW) in 1882, it decided to enlarge its Stratford operation even more, and in 1888–89 it relocated much of the GW equipment from the GW's former headquarters in Hamilton to Stratford. By then, Stratford had evolved into a key railway hub with lines that led to Goderich, Southampton, Wiarton, Sarnia, Windsor, and Lake Erie. Vast yards sprawled to include a roundhouse,

repair shops, a nursery for station gardens along the line, and a popular Railway YMCA. The brick station stood two storeys tall and could once claim an impressive tower.

In 1907, more enlargements began at the shops until two years later the work area measured an incredible 30,000 square metres or 320,000 square feet. In 1926, the CNR closed the former Canadian Northern (CNo) facilities in Leaside and relocated them to Stratford as well. Still more expansions occurred in 1948–49.

But just a decade later, with the CNR's dieselization nearly complete, it began to close down much of the Stratford operation. Cooper Bessemer bought what remained until finally, in 1964, the shops fell silent for good.[3]

A new YMCA now occupies the site of the original, while the nursery is long gone. The station serves far fewer trains these days thanks to federal cutbacks to VIA Rail, but still remains an impressive building. A short distance west of the station, the vast CN shops have survived (at least into 2013). This massive building measures 220 metres (790 feet) long with two wings of 180 metres (500 feet) each. Despite a fire in 2003, the building houses a variety of uses, but remains in peril of demolition. In 2010, the City of Stratford began the process of acquiring the building, but as of 2013 had yet to advance that process. Portions of the structure have been renovated and now form part of the University of Waterloo's Stratford campus.

TRENTON

The former Central Ontario Railway (COR) roundhouse in Trenton, likely built in 1911, when the Canadian Northern assumed the COR, is now the "Roundhouse on Dufferin" and contains a number of commercial tenants. Although it retains its overall shape, there have been many alterations to accommodate the needs of its businesses.

TORONTO

With its situation as a harbour and its role as provincial capital, Toronto quickly rose to become Ontario's main industrial and railway hub. From its quiet beginnings in a wooden "union" station on Lake Ontario, Toronto's railway network became the focus of an international network of rail lines. Many had their own stations and roundhouses as well as coal chutes and water towers.

Until the 1980s major roundhouses still survived at Lambton, Spadina, and John Street, while the East Toronto yard had originally contained a variety of railway structures, including a coach house, a Railway YMCA, roundhouse, and a vast network of sidings. Today VIA Rail and GO Transit operate on the only three remaining East Toronto tracks, and the former yard area has become a community of condominium town houses. A similar fate befell the Canadian National Railway's Spadina roundhouse and yards with a forest of condominium towers and the Rogers Centre now on the site.

The Grand Trunk yards, which spawned the town of New Toronto, now house the storage and repair facilities for both GO and VIA, although few heritage structures remain among them. A short distance west of the yards, where the Canadian Pacific Railway (CPR) alignment bends northward, a switching tower still remains.

Despite the loss of much of its railway heritage, Toronto has, after many years of typical political procrastination, gained what is arguably Ontario's best-preserved roundhouse in a park festooned with much railway history. These are found in Roundhouse Park, centred on the CPR John Street roundhouse.

The first roundhouse at John Street was built in 1897 by the CPR and contained fifteen stalls, with more added between 1907 and 1918. In 1928, the old roundhouse was proving inadequate, and by 1931 the CPR had opened a new brick structure capable of handling thirty-two locomotives. Its 40-metre (120-foot) turntable was built by the Canadian Bridge Company. The building offered such new features as direct steaming from the Toronto Terminal Railway's heating plant. With the newly opened Union Station nearby, the yards saw more than forty trains a day steam in and out.

More than forty various structures made up the John Street facility and covered 16 acres, providing work for more than 150 men.

Then, in the 1960s when both the Canadian National Railway (CNR) and Canadian Pacific

Railway (CPR) opened larger and more modern facilities north of Toronto, the two lines closed their respective roundhouses. While that of the CNR at Spadina was demolished in 1986 to make way for the Rogers Centre, the John Street roundhouse was donated to the City of Toronto to use as a railway museum, a project that took two decades to accomplish. Much of the credit is owed to the hard-working volunteers of the Toronto Railway Historical Society, which has established a museum in one-third of the building and brought in a variety of railway equipment and buildings to what is now called "Roundhouse Park." Here too stands the little turreted wooden Don station, a large coal chute, and the water tower, painted in the colours of the Steamwhistle Brewery, which was the first tenant in the roundhouse. A more recent tenant is a Leon's furniture showroom, which has preserved the high ceiling and windows.

Toronto's historic CPR John Street roundhouse is now the focus of the popular railway display in Roundhouse Park.

But Toronto remains an active rail hub as well, with the historic Union Station and companion Fairmont Royal York Hotel, as well as functioning switching towers at Cherry Street, Yonge Street, and west of Union Station. All are constructed of brick, stand two storeys tall, and were built with the completion of grade separation work in the 1920s. An older wooden switching tower that formerly stood by Bathurst Street now forms part of the Roundhouse Park display.

While many of the city's industrial spurs have been removed, they have left behind a legacy of railway buildings. One of the most praised is the Queens Quay Terminal on the city's Harbourfront. Here, in 1926, the New York firm of Moores and Dunford designed a six-storey cold storage terminal where produce arriving by ship could be stored pending transshipment onto trains or trucks.

The concrete art deco warehouse with its prominent clock tower contained not only ice making facilities but deluxe offices and small manufacturing operations such as the Canadian Doughnut Company. Trains would back in through the high front doorway, while trucks would line up at the side. The ingenious train-loading system allowed more than 130 tonnes of ice to be placed daily on the Canadian National and Canadian Pacific trains to provide the railways' only source of refrigeration at the time. In 1983, the terminal was converted into award-winning offices, stores, and condos, and is a key visual and functional focus for the waterfront.

So prominent were the railways in Toronto that the Canadian National Exhibition dedicated a building exclusively to them. George W. Guinlock designed the structure in 1907. Three prominent domed areas each featured displays of the province's three major rail lines, the Canadian Pacific Railway, the Grand Trunk, and the Canadian Northern Railway. By 1968, railways had lost much of their importance and the building became the Music Building. After a fire in 1987, it later reopened as a CNE Seniors Centre and archives and now houses the Sustainable Condo Exhibit.

THUNDER BAY ORE DOCK

By the early 1900s, Port Arthur and Fort William had become Canada's leading grain ports. The long strings of the grain silos yet loom above the piers that line the waterfront, many now vacant.

But one outstanding port structure is the old ore dock. This high, orange-coloured structure was built in 1945 to ship out iron ore hauled in by the Canadian National Railway (CNR) from the Steep Rock Mine in Atikokan. A high trestle rose from the CNR tracks to cross the streets and access the dock. Shipping ended in the 1970s and the trestle dismantled in the 1990s. Although silent, the ore dock still looms large in the history of the community, and in 2011 was added to Thunder Bay's heritage registry. In 2012, plans to redevelop the structure were being discussed.

NORTH BAY T&NO OFFICES

By 1908, the Temiskaming and Northern Ontario Railway (T&NO) had reached its junction with the National Transcontinental Railway (NTR) at Cochrane. During that period it was replacing many of its first-generation stations with more elaborate structures, especially those at Cobalt, where the silver boom had created a new town of 10,000, and at Temagami where the new stone station was drawing tourists to the waters of Lake Temagami.

In North Bay, the T&NO hired the firm of H.W. Angus to design their new offices. This elegant white limestone structure was opened in 1908, measured 15 metres by 30 metres, and housed twenty-one offices between its three floors. This Château-style building is marked by two styles of stonework which emphasized the corners and windows. A three-storey gable rises from the front entrance, while dormers appear around the roof of the building. Located at Oak and Regina Streets, today it houses ONtel, and is considered one of Ontario's grandest railway offices.[4]

GRAIN ELEVATORS AND FEED MILLS

While the grain elevator remains the enduring iconic, albeit vanishing, symbol of the prairies' railway legacy, that heritage has vanished almost entirely from Ontario. Yet, for the first three decades of this province's railway history, grain elevators were a prominent trackside fixture. But by the 1880s, western Canada's grain lands had opened a new opportunity for grain growers, and Ontario's farm economy switched to livestock. With this shift, grain elevators became obsolete and were either converted to or replaced with feed mills. But since feed mills were for the most part a local service, few required a trackside location. Still, a few trackside mills and elevators loom over the tracks, now one of the forgotten features of Ontario's railway legacy.

The grain elevator in Pontypool, which is identical in style to those on the prairies, was built in 1918 and stands by the tracks of the Canadian Pacific Railway's Ontario and Quebec (O&Q) rail line. It was donated by the CPR to the Friends of the Pontypool Elevator, which has undertaken some basic repairs, although no re-use has yet occurred.

Unionville's Stiver Feed Mill, adjacent to the preserved station, operated between 1910 and 1968, after having served originally as a grain elevator. The town of Markham purchased the heritage structure in 1993, and today it belongs to the Unionville Village Conservancy. Plans were launched in 2010 to allocate $150,000 to stabilize the mill and open a granary and chocolate emporium, which will include historical information.

The oldest of the railway grain elevators is the Currie elevator in Port Perry. Shortly after the Whitby and Port Perry Railway opened its line in 1874, grain merchant George Currie and his brother began to construct the elevator. This solid structure used planks on the lower 10 metres, which measure

2 inches by 8 inches and 2 inches by 6 inches on the upper levels. The building measures nearly 30 metres high and was the only building in town to escape the flames of an 1883 fire that destroyed the main street. The tracks were lifted in the 1940s and the station moved across the street. In 1981, an auto supply company moved into the building, which is now a designated heritage structure.

In 1909, on a branch of the Toronto, Grey and Bruce line, which led into Durham, a feed mill was built to ship oats across Canada. Following a fire, it was rebuilt as a feed mill and today stands beside the Heritage Walkway Bridge, a former railway bridge.

Stouffville's 1922 Reesor Elevator, although now a designated heritage building, is threatened with removal by GO Transit, which owns the property.

Other heritage grain elevators and feed mills across Ontario include those in Monkton, built on the 1908 Canadian Pacific Railway (CPR) line

The former Pontypool grain elevator is one of the few survivors of the days when such structures were trackside fixtures.

to Goderich; Claremont, on the CPR's Ontario and Quebec line; and Prairie Siding, which offers visitors a prairie-like vista along the Canadian National Railway track. Dundalk, Newmarket, Jarvis, Camlachie, and Nashville also still retain their heritage grain elevators and feed mills. Various newer feed mills and grain silos still function at existing and former rail side locations, especially throughout southwestern Ontario.

CELEBRATING THE HERITAGE:

THE RAILWAY MUSEUMS

Heritage lovers in Ontario have found many ways to celebrate and cherish their railway heritage. They have moved station houses to parks and museums, they have preserved old locomotives, and they have created websites. But the most compelling are the railway museums.

NORTHERN ONTARIO RAILROAD MUSEUM AND HERITAGE CENTRE, CAPREOL

What better place to create a full-fledged railway museum than in a full-fledged railway town. Capreol sprang to life as a major divisional town on the Canadian Northern Railway. Here, north of Sudbury, the Canadian Northern (CNo) built a large two-storey station with passenger facilities and offices, a roundhouse, water tower, and coal chute, while nearby a Railway YMCA provided comfortable accommodation for the train crews. Closeby was the home of the CNo superintendent, and it is here that the Northern Ontario Railroad Museum is housed. Inside displays depict the early days of Capreol and of the vanished mining town of Sellwood.

Outside, in Prescott Park, the collection of historical equipment includes the Canadian National Railway's 4-8-2 Bullet Nose Betty #6077 steam locomotive, the first of the equipment to arrive in 1967. Behind it are the engine's tender, a Pullman coach, baggage car, cabooses, and a reconstructed school car. A rare piece is the last of the slag cars from the massive Inco refinery near Sudbury. A boxcar converted to a home reveals the harsh conditions of those who during the depression could not find proper housing. In 2012, the museum successfully bid on a much smaller 2-6-0 Temiskaming and Northern Ontario Railway locomotive #219 from the Ontario Northland Railway yards in Cochrane.

COCHRANE RAILWAY AND PIONEER MUSEUM, COCHRANE

Located fittingly beside Cochrane's century-old train station, and the Ontario Northland Railway's main yards, this museum display, created in 1970, is headed by historic steam locomotive #137, built in Kingston in 1913 and last used on the ONR's Centennial Train in 1967. Behind the engine,

The CNR's Bullet Nose Betty leads the way beside Chapleau's Northern Ontario Railroad Museum and Heritage Centre.

baggage car 8868, built in 1929, displays stories of the area's local history, while passenger coach 5069, dating from 1924, focuses on railway heritage and features original seats and a model railway layout.

RON MOREL MEMORIAL MUSEUM, KAPUSKASING

Situated beside Kapuskasing's handsome brick-on-stone Canadian National Railway (CNR) station, the railway display includes a CNR 4-6-2 steam locomotive #1507, built in 1919. Behind it are a Pullman sleeper, built in 1913, and a former colonist car, which dates from 1919. The museum is named in honour of the local historian whose enthusiasm and dedication brought the museum into existence.

SMITHS FALLS RAILWAY MUSEUM

The focus of this extensive railway museum is the magnificent Smiths Falls Canadian Northern Railway station. Built in 1914, it is brick-on-stone with an octagonal tower rising through the roof above the operator's bay window. A large porte cochère welcomed travellers on the street side. When passenger service ended in 1979, the station began to crumble with water damage to the roof and a collapsed floor. The usual vandalism hadn't helped either. But in 1983, the Smiths Falls Railway

Museum Association sprang into action, not only restoring the station but accumulating a remarkable array of railway buildings and equipment.

In front of the station stands an ex-Canadian Pacific Railway diesel engine S-3 #6501 in its traditional maroon and grey colours and dating from 1957. Behind the station resides a 4-6-0 steam locomotive # 1112, built in 1912 for the Canadian Northern Railway (CNo). In tow and nearby are four coaches and a rare dental car used by the Canadian National Railway. It dates originally from 1913, when the CNo built it as a sleeper car. Visitors can also view a Cadillac inspection car. Buildings have been moved onto the site as well, including the octagonal former station shelter from Nolans — which began life as a water tower — and a one-time section house.

CANADIAN MUSEUM OF SCIENCE AND TECHNOLOGY, OTTAWA

This sprawling complex places Canada's railway heritage in the context of its technological role, and not just a nostalgic role. Sadly, the museum's collection is simply too vast to put it all on display. But it does show off the cream of its collection.

Most visitors head for the locomotive room to see four giant steam locomotives, especially the Canadian National Railway's streamlined 4-8-4 #6400, built in 1935, the first streamlined engine in Canada, and the one that pulled the 1939 Royal Train through Ontario. Beside it, the Canadian Pacific Railway's 4-8-4 #3100, built in 1928, was used on the overnight trains between Toronto and Montreal. The CPR's #2858 is the newest of the steam display built in 1938. All three remained in use as late as 1966. The oldest locomotive on display was built in 1911 for the CPR.

On the grounds outside, the hard working Bytown Railway Society has assembled a wide variety of equipment, including coaches, cranes, boom cars, and spreaders.

HALTON COUNTY RADIAL RAILWAY AND STREETCAR MUSEUM, GUELPH

Located down a country road near Guelph, Ontario, the Halton County Radial Railway and Streetcar Museum shows how hard work and dedication can pay off. The efforts all began in 1953 at a New Year's Eve party when five streetcar lovers began to discuss the pending closing of the TTC's small, historic streetcar collection. Focusing on preserving the largest of the streetcars, they acquired a property, ironically on what had been

Visitors can enjoy a ride in an interurban radial streetcar at the Halton County Radial Railway and Streetcar Museum near Rockwood.

an actual radial streetcar line — that of the Toronto Suburban Railway, which ran from Toronto to Guelph. By June of 1954, TTC streetcars 1326 and 2210 had found a new home.

As the years passed, the growing group of volunteers laid more track and erected a car barn. They also added more than forty pieces of equipment, including open streetcars and interurban cars complete with their wood panelling, plush seats, and separate smoking compartments. A pair of original red TTC subway cars arrived as well. In fact, more than passenger cars are displayed here. There are several pieces of utilitarian working equipment as well, such as snow ploughs and cranes, and a small fleet of historical buses.

A newly constructed display barn allows visitors to walk through much of the collection and then ride an open streetcar, a once familiar Witt, and a radial car from the Montreal and Southern Counties Railway. The tram rides follow the original Toronto and Suburban (T&S) right of way to a floral garden and the Meadowvale radial shelter from the T&S line. The relocated Rockwood Grand Trunk station offers a display of early photos and railway artifacts.

CHATHAM RAILWAY MUSEUM, CHATHAM

Located across the tracks from Chatham's grand VIA Rail station, the Chatham Railway Museum is housed in a 1955 Canadian National Railway baggage car. The displays include railway uniforms and equipment, a model railway, and a children's area.

ELGIN COUNTY RAILWAY MUSEUM, ST. THOMAS

It is little wonder that St. Thomas calls itself "Railway City," for not only can it boast of having preserved and restored one of Ontario's largest abandoned railway stations, but offers one of its most extensive railway museum collections.

Besides the station, one of the few buildings to survive the demise of the city's railways is the Michigan Central Railway's 1913 shops. From its start in 1988, the museum has gone on to acquire a 1917 London and Port Stanley radial streetcar, a 1957 Canadian Pacific Railway diesel electric locomotive, and the star attraction, the Canadian National Railway's 1937 4-6-4 steam locomotive # 5700, which was capable of racing at 100 miles per hour on its Toronto to Montreal run. A sleeper, baggage car, and various boxcars and cabooses round out the display. A gift shop and model railway layout are located inside.

Down the track, the museum has also preserved a switching tower. Resting beside the massive car shop are the two incline railway cars that carried tourists up and down the steep hillsides of Port Stanley from the hotels to the dance halls and the beach.

The Elgin County Railway Museum has preserved many pieces of railway equipment including the CNR's locomotive #5700.

FORT ERIE RAILWAY MUSEUM, FORT ERIE

Fort Erie is another once-dominant railway centre, where the only evidence of its heyday are its yards and the Fort Erie Railway Museum. Equipment includes the Canadian National Railway's 4-8-4 steam locomotive #6218, and a caboose. A diminutive Porter 0-4-0 30-inch gauge locomotive is located here as well. A gift shop and admission office are located inside the Grand Trunk's 1871 bridge station, while the main displays appear inside the much grander Ridgeway station, built by the GT in 1900. Throughout the refurbished interior are displays of railway artifacts, photographs, and a model railway layout. Fort Erie's passenger stations, those built by the GT in a witch's hat style, and by the Michigan Central in a simple wooden structure, were removed after passenger service ended. The now-reduced yards are located nearby.

MEMORY JUNCTION MUSEUM, BRIGHTON

Just when Ralph Bangay was looking for someplace to store his extensive collection of Brighton's memorabilia, the Canadian National Railway (CNR) station came up for sale. For $400 he purchased the threatened 1857 structure and ended up creating one of Ontario's finer railway museums. Inside the brick station he has placed much railway equipment, timetables, photographs, books, and other archival material, while outside he and his volunteers assembled a train set that includes a 1906 Grand Trunk 2-8-0 steam locomotive #2534, rescued from vandalism in a Belleville park, along with two boxcars, a flat car, and three cabooses. Here too, both CN Rail and the Canadian Pacific Railway main lines are busy with frequent freights and VIA Rail's passenger trains.

KOMOKA RAILWAY MUSEUM, KOMOKA

Focusing on the former Komoka train station, moved from its original site nearby, the museum offers a 1913 50-ton Shay steam logging locomotive, stored inside, while outside sits a 1939 Canadian National Railway baggage car and caboose. Among the collection are jiggers, lamps, and various railway tools. The small station shelter from Longwoods is a rare surviving example of an early Grand Trunk shelter.

SCHREIBER RAILWAY ARRAY MUSEUM, SCHREIBER

In recognition of its railway heritage, that of an important Canadian Pacific Railway (CPR) divisional town, the community of Schreiber has completed the Schreiber Railway Array Museum — a railway display with a 1956 CPR boxcar, a flat car, and baggage car, which contains historic displays of railway and community memorabilia. The fleet is headed up by a CPR diesel built in 1955 and numbered 6539. A miniature replica of the town's Railway YMCA has been built in front of the display, which sits across the vast rail yards from the historic station.

THE SCHOOL ON WHEELS, CLINTON

From the late 1920s until the mid-1960s, children in the remote regions of northern Ontario did not travel to school, their school travelled to them. During that period before highways penetrated the north, the Ontario government along with the Canadian National Railway (CNR), the Canadian Pacific Railway (CPR), and the Temiskaming and Northern Ontario Railway (T&NO) transformed seven passenger coaches into travelling classrooms, complete with desks, books, chalkboards, and even a small apartment for the teacher. When a former student noticed that his old classroom was up for sale, he contacted the people of Clinton, Ontario, the hometown of Fred Sloman, who had taught in the school car for forty-two years. The town worked to bring the historic classroom to Clinton, where they have restored it to the school car that those former students might remember. It has since become an iconic and popular attraction for tourists and present-day students alike

ROUNDHOUSE PARK AND THE TORONTO RAILWAY MUSEUM, TORONTO

Finally, Toronto has its railway museum. Having been a railway hub since 1853, when the first steam engine puffed away to Aurora (then Machell's Corners), Toronto has displayed little of its railway heritage, and what did exist was widely scattered.

Fred Sloman's former school car is now a museum in his hometown of Clinton, where he taught and lived in this apartment for forty-two years.

The Don station sat in Leaside's Todmorden Park, the Canadian National's former steam engine, #6213 languished in the Exhibition grounds, while coal chutes, switching towers, and a water tower sat deteriorating near the CN Tower.

In 1986, the Canadian Pacific Railway (CPR) moved out of the roundhouse and donated it to the city for a railway museum. But, typically, Toronto politicians and bureaucrats continued to ignore the potential to celebrate the city's vital railway heritage. Finally, in 1997, the Toronto Railway Historical Association began to assemble what has become one of Ontario's premier railway museums.

The main attraction is the former CPR roundhouse, built between 1929 and 1931, replacing an earlier structure. This 9,300 square-metre structure could boast thirty-two stalls for locomotives and a 40-metre (120-foot) turntable. Most of the forty-three buildings and other structures are now gone from the site, but others have moved in. The little turreted Don station now resides here, as do a pair of cabins formerly located in the Bathurst Street yards, while the historic water tower and coal chute round out the complex.

Sharing the roundhouse itself are the popular Steamwhistle Brewery, a Leon's store, and the collection of the Toronto Railway Historical Association, including work cars, boxcars, and a rare vinegar car that dates back to 1938. CN Rail's 1942 4-8-4 steam locomotive, # 6213, now resides here, as does the CPR's Cape Race, a 1928 official coach. Lurking under the coal chute is a 1950 diesel, #2637.

During the summer children may ride a miniature train, while their parents can visit a model railway layout.

Roundhouse Park and Railway Museum in Toronto has many structures and pieces of railway equipment on display, including the CNR's #4308, resting beneath a coal chute.

But Toronto's love-hate relationship with its railway history has not entirely subsided, as in 2012 Toronto Hydro ordered the museum to move out of the portion of the roundhouse controlled by that corporation.

PRIVATE MUSEUMS

Ontario's love of the rails does not end at public museums. Many enthusiasts have assembled a railway heritage that remains private, although visits can be arranged. Near Uptergrove, Ontario, Cecil Byers has assembled a small collection of railway equipment, including four boxcars and two cabooses, along with various signalling devices. For a number of years a small 0-4-0 steam locomotive, originally from the Sir Adam Beck generating station at Niagara Falls, rested among them before finding a new home at the Niagara Falls Railway Museum. Contrary to its name, the museum is not actually in Niagara Falls at all, but rather is housed in a grouping of old railway shops tucked away in Fort Erie. That collection, not currently open to the public, also includes three former Canadian Pacific Railway boxcars, rule books, tools, and a collection of "motorcars" or jiggers.

Near Thamesford, the Valleyview Railroad museum has assembled a couple of cabooses to go with the former Thorndale Canadian National Railway station.

RAILWAY EQUIPMENT DISPLAYS

While many railway displays don't qualify as museums, they nonetheless contribute to the celebration of Ontario's railway heritage. While cabooses are so ubiquitous they do not form part of this chapter, many engines, coaches, and train sets do share in that celebration.

In 1963, when clearing a road near Atikokan in northwestern Ontario, the Ministry of Natural Resources unearthed an abandoned Shay steam locomotive that had worked for the Shevlin Clark Lumber Company and was built in 1913. It had languished in the bush since 1924 and today sits in the Atikokan Civic Centre Museum and Historic Park.

For many years, the Collingwood Canadian National Railway (CNR) station had housed the community's museum. When it was discovered that the building was no longer adequate for that purpose, it was torn down and replaced with a replica of the original Grand Trunk (GT) building. On a track nearby, three CNR boxcars serve as information and display centres.

Although Goderich can boast of two handsome and historic railway stations and a massive railway bridge, the only historic equipment is tucked away safely inside the Huron County Museum and it is a Canadian Pacific Railway (CPR) 0-6-0 steam locomotive that dates from 1913.

Across the tracks from the historic Guelph GT

station, and behind a chain-link fence, rests the CNR's 1940 4-8-4 steam locomotive #6167.

Well out of sight, at least for most, are four former coaches from the "Smoky Falls" Railway, more correctly known as the Spruce Falls Power and Paper Company Railway. This long-lost line connected the pulp mills in Kapuskasing with a hydro town at Smoky Falls. The old coaches rest on the former right-of-way, well to the north of Kapuskasing, and serve as a fishing camp.

Haliburton was once the destination for the Victoria Railway from Lindsay. Just west of the historic station is the Grand Trunk's 1911 2-8-0 steam locomotive #2616, one of the last to run on the line. By the station itself, a caboose and boxcar round out the railway display.

Who doesn't enjoy a winery visit? At Puddicome's Estate Farms and Winery near Winona, visitors can also view historic railway equipment, as the estate boasts three former Procor tank cars, a 1907 caboose, which contains overnight accommodation, and a 1925 Pullman sleeper car. Rides are available on a miniature train, which departs from the relocated Canadian Pacific Railway (CPR) Summerville station.

Although the Kawartha Lakes town of Lindsay was once a key rail hub for central Ontario, there remains not a metre of track, nor any original railway structure. Rather, the celebration of the town's railway heritage rests in Memorial Park at the south end of the town and consists of a 1951

CNR diesel locomotive, a pair of boxcars, and formerly a caboose, which was badly damaged by an arsonist (who was caught and charged). In 2009, the historic Toronto, Hamilton and Buffalo (TH&B) 0-6-0 steam engine #42 was released from its hiding place inside an old mill beside the canal and brought to Memorial Park, where it will form the focus of a proposed railway heritage centre for the town.

The Western Fair Grounds of London, Ontario, has on outside display a 1910 GT 2-6-0 steam locomotive #86.

Adjacent to the Aultsville Grand Trunk (GT) station, rescued from the town, which was flooded by the St. Lawrence Seaway, is a train display that includes a 1910 GT 2-6-0 stream locomotive #1008, a 1923 CNR baggage car and a 1901 GT coach, all on an original section of track.

An iconic sight on Highway 11 north of Orillia is Weber's restaurant. It is a must-stop for cottagers en route to Muskoka. The grounds include an extensive display of railway equipment, which includes two dining cars, including a one-time CNR dining car last operated by VIA Rail as a day-nighter, and several boxcars, along with a caboose. Unfortunately, the VIA car's gold and blue colours have been obscured by a coating of grey paint.

Much of northern Ontario is steeped in railway history, especially that of Rainy River. Here the Canadian Northern Railway crossed into

Minnesota on a large through truss bridge. The large brick station has been saved from the CNR and houses municipal offices. Nearby rests a massive 2-10-2 1916 steam locomotive, retired in 1958 as CNR #4008, along with a former CNR baggage car and caboose.

A popular sight in the former rail yards of Palmerston, where the Grand Trunk (GT) station has been restored, is the last steam engine to operate in these yards and that is the GT's 1910 2-6-0 steam locomotive #81.

Although it is nowhere near Sarnia's magnificent Grand Trunk station designed by Joseph Hobson, the CNR's 1944 4-8-2 #6069 steam locomotive is on prominent display in Bayview Park near Point Edward, and is one of the first things travellers see after crossing the Bluewater Bridge and exiting from Highway 402. Point Edward was the original terminus for the Grand Trunk

Until it closed in 2011, the Ossawippi Express Restaurant in Orillia consisted of a rare collection of historic coaches. The collection included a

A former VIA Rail streamliner train set is on display in Thunder Bay's Kaministiquia Heritage Park.

1915 interurban coach from the London and Port Stanley Railway, a pair of CPR official cars, and an 1896 Pullman business car, the Nova Scotia, as well as a pair of early baggage cars and a boxcar. All had been connected together to create the restaurant.

Regrettably, the city showed no interest in retaining any of them. A developer, Skyline International Development, preparing a resort and condo development at Port McNicoll, concluded that at least a couple of the coaches would perfectly complement the heritage theme they were proposing for the site. That theme includes replicating the CPR's railway station and returning the CPR's 1907 cruise ship S.S. *Keewatin* from Michigan, where it had been docked since its retirement in 1966, to its home base beside the Port McNicoll dock. That mighty vessel returned in June 2012, and by September had opened for tours.

Thunder Bay has assembled a 1954 streamliner train set in the Kaministiquia River Heritage Park, only a short distance from the historic CPR station. Resplendent in VIA's blue and gold colour scheme, it consists of a 1954 FP9 streamliner diesel locomotive plus a café lounge, a coach, and a sleeper. It forms part of a riverside walkway where the hundred-year-old tug, the *James Whalen*, is also on display.

In the Dundas Valley Conservation Area, the trail head for the Hamilton to Brantford rail trail, lies in a replica of the Grimsby Grand Trunk station, a turreted wooden building that was destroyed by fire in the 1990s. While the interior of the building is a mere two decades old, it is designed to remind the visitor of an early wood-lined waiting room. Outside, a railway display includes the CPR's 1928 Manitoban official car, and 1931 baggage car.

— 9 —

ALL ABOARD:

ONTARIO'S LIVING RAILWAY HERITAGE

When, in August of 2012, Ontario's then-Northern Development Minister, Rick Bartolucci, shocked Ontario by suddenly and without consultation cancelling the *Northlander* train from Toronto to Cochrane, he ended not just an era but a train ride that revealed an Ontario that few southerners even knew.

For the *Northlander* was to Ontario what VIA Rail's cross country *Canadian* is to Canada. It revealed to its passengers a geographical and historical cross-section of the province from the urban sprawl of the GTA, through the rolling farmlands of the Oak Ridges Moraine, the rugged rocks of the Canadian Shield, into the far northeast with its mining boom towns and its clay belts, before finally reaching the Artic watershed.

The *Northlander* also formed a vital part of northern Ontario's heritage. To Northerners, cancelling the train was what demolishing old city hall would be to Torontonians. Although no other rail experience can compare to that on the *Northlander*, many offer a trip back in time, or in some cases, a trip to the future.

THE POLAR BEAR EXPRESS

At least Bartolucci retained the Ontario Northland Railway's popular *Polar Bear Express*, linking Cochrane with Moosonee. For this train brings considerable tourist revenue to the motels and inns of Cochrane, including an inn on the second floor of the historic station, but even more so to the hardscrabble community of Moosonee.

The original purpose of the link, however, was to tap into lignite deposits and to open a salt water port on James Bay, which it reached in 1932. The site was beset by the fickle shifting sand bars in the Moose River, and the dream of a port was never realized.

But the tourists came, curious to experience Ontario's remote north country and to visit the remains of Ontario's oldest non-native settlement, the 1673 Hudson's Bay fur post of Moose Factory Island.

The *Polar Bear Express*, combined now with what was the local *Little Bear*, makes for an all-day return trip through the swamp, muskeg, and the

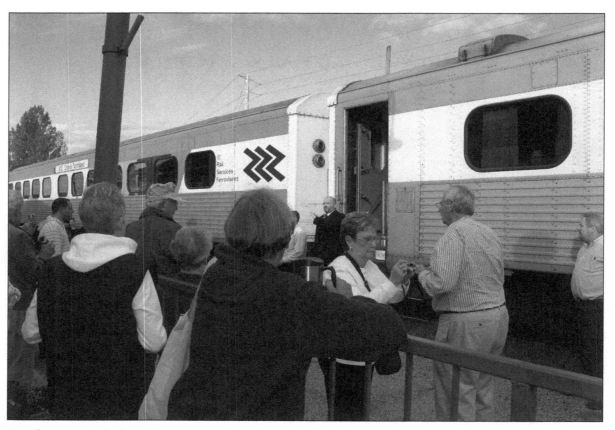

Crowds turn out at the Gravenhurst station in September 2012 to bid a final farewell to the ONR's Northlander.

flat forests of spruce and tamarack of the Hudson Bay lowlands. Small communities appear by the track, places with names like Fraserdale and Coral Rapids, with its tiny log station shelter. Much of the route follows the valley of the Albany River, where two massive hydro dams, at Island Falls, built in 1925, and at Otter Rapids, built in 1958, are visible from the train. The view from the 550-metre long Moose River bridge provides a welcome and scenic break in what is often called the world's largest swamp.

For the few First Nations villages that line the route, the train is their sole link to the outside, as it largely is for Moosonee itself. This Cree community of 2,000 consists of basic housing and an even more basic main street. However, the newer Christ the King Roman Catholic Cathedral, built in 1946, offers a series of stunning stained glass windows. Designed in 1987 by Cree artist Keena, the windows depict the Cree version of the Christmas story and include a depiction of Kateri Tekakwitha, a Mohawk born in 1656 who was elevated to sainthood in 2012.[1]

When the train arrives, most passengers make for the river about half a kilometre from the station, where a fleet of Cree freighter canoes waits to ferry them to Moose Factory Island only a few minutes away. Most of Moose Factory Island resembles a fairly modern town, with housing, community centres, and an arena. The main employer is the Weeneebayko hospital, which serves the James Bay coastal communities and offers housing for its sizable staff.

The Hudson's Bay Company historical area includes a cemetery; a staff house dating from 1847; and St. Thomas Anglican church, built in 1885 (with holes drilled into the floors to prevent it from floating away during the annual spring floods), as well as carpenter's house and servant's house, all of which date from the 1800s. The blacksmith shop dates back to 1849, while the stone powder magazine was built in 1865.

Overnight stays are available in Moosonee at one of two local lodges, a handful of B&Bs, but especially at the newly opened and Cree-run Ecolodge, situated on Moose Factory Island itself.

During the busier tourist season, entertainment on board the *Polar Bear Express* helps to pass the dark hours of the return trip.

AGAWA CANYON

One of Ontario's best-known train experiences is the world renowned Agawa Canyon train. Operated now by CN Rail, it began with the Algoma Central Railway, which was founded in 1899 by Frances Clergue to haul ore from the mines at Wawa, as well as the rich harvest of timber.

But the beauties of Algoma country didn't remain unknown for long. In the 1920s the artist's collective known as the Group of Seven often boarded the train to paint Algoma's soaring peaks with their brilliant fall colours and the wind-whipped clouds of fall and winter, and would often stay for days or weeks.

Since that time, the trip has drawn visitors from around the world. Today, the lengthy train departs from downtown Sault Ste. Marie beside a modern and comfortable station. Passengers can enjoy fine food in the dining car, and listen to a GPS-triggered commentary. Video screens connected to the front of the engine reveal the view that the engineers themselves see, especially as the train soars over the mighty Bellevue and the Montreal River trestles.

The layover in the Agawa Canyon allows time to hike the trails or to climb to a lookout high above the canyon. For those who want to replicate the Group of Seven experience, a caboose has been retrofitted as a small cottage, complete with beds, and propane-powered stove heater and lighting. It is hauled to a siding in Agawa Canyon where its guests hike, paint, or fish, all within the remote tranquility and splendour of the Agawa Canyon.

CN's local train pauses for passengers at Hawk Junction, en route from Sault Ste. Marie to Hearst on what was once the ACR.

Three times a week a local train follows the historic route from the Soo all the way to Hearst. Along the way the train stops to board fishers, canoers, and tourists at Hawk Junction with its busy brick station. North of that, however, the route has no road access until approaching Hearst. On the way, it stops at remote lodges and cottages, passing aging ghost towns and crossing lakes. One unusual crossing is that over Oba Lake on a floating bridge.

THE HUNTSVILLE AND LAKE OF BAYS RAILWAY

This short rail ride replicates a route that was never long to begin with. Beginning in 1900, from the train station in Huntsville, steamers like the Algonquin would carry vacationers through Fairy Lake to North Portage on Peninsula Lake. Known as the world's shortest railway, the Portage Flyer would then carry the passengers, freight, and mail up a grade of 80 metres, for a distance of about 3 kilometres, to South Portage on Lake of Bays, where more steamers waited to carry them to such resorts as the Britannia Inn, Wa Wa Hotel, or Bigwin Inn.

The arrival of the highways in the 1950s and the popularity of cottages over the resorts ended the life of the rail line and the steamers. The train ceased operation in 1959.

After spending a number of years in Pinnafore Park in St. Thomas, the original engines were brought back to Huntsville in 1984, where through the hard work of dedicated volunteers they returned to action in 1995. The two steam engines were built in 1926 and hauled the portage flyer between 1933 and the day it ceased to operate. The open trams date from 1894 when they were acquired by the Huntsville and Lake of Bays Railway from the cities of Toronto and Atlanta, respectively. A 1949 diesel-powered switcher helps with the motive power whenever the steam engines are not operating.

Today's journeys begin from the purpose-built "Village Station" adjacent to the Muskoka Pioneer Village at the Muskoka Heritage Place in Huntsville, from there it follows the banks of the Muskoka River to the shore of Fairy Lake. There, the historic purser's cabin from Norway Point on Lake of Bays serves as the "station," where the engine changes ends for the return journey. The "Village Station" not only contains the H&LOB ticket office, but also railway images, artifacts, and an operating telegraph key, and serves as a meeting hall as well.

THE YORK AND DURHAM HERITAGE RAILWAY

After the Canadian National Railway (CNR) shut down its line to Coboconk in the 1960s, tracks remained in place as far as Uxbridge. The Toronto and Nipissing Railway was initiated by William Gooderham, owner of the Gooderham and Worts Distillery on Parliament Street in Toronto, and was intended to carry grain to provide his raw material.

Service to Uxbridge began in 1871 and was later extended to Coboconk, but never reached the destination of Lake Nipissing envisioned in its name. In the 1880s, the line became part of the Midland Railway and shortly thereafter of the Grand Trunk. The CNR ended service to Coboconk in the 1960s. When the railway no longer needed the trackage between Stouffville and Uxbridge, the CNR set it aside for future GO train operations. In 1986, a group of local enthusiasts introduced the York and Durham Heritage Railway (Y&DHR), named after the two regions through which it runs, to encourage tourism to Uxbridge and Stouffville.

Although it has no steam, the three vintage diesel locomotives date from the mid-1950s, and represent the early days of diesel motive power. The oldest is #1310, which began service on the Ontario Northland Railway (ONR) in 1951, #22 was built in 1955 for the Roberval and Saguenay Railway in Quebec, while #3612 began life with the Duluth, Winnipeg, and Pacific Railway in 1956. Based in the yards at Uxbridge, the Y&DHR also owns four coaches, the oldest of which dates from 1919 when it was built for the Canadian Northern as a colonist car. A former Canadian Pacific Railway (CPR) coach dates from 1929, with the others being more recent, dating from the 1950s. It has not been without its own challenges, such as when residents of a newly completed subdivision in Uxbridge built beside the rail line complained that there were trains on the track.

When operating, the trains travel twice daily between the recently built station in Stouffville to the Grand Trunk's historic 1904 "witch's hat" station, where travellers can visit the railway's museum display. On special occasions, such as Doors Open events, the train may travel to the original and now-restored Toronto and Nipissing station in Markham.

THE SOUTH SIMCOE RAILWAY

For railway historians, this is the "real McCoy." Here, on a short section of track between its home base of Tottenham and Beeton, an 1883 4-4-0 Canadian Pacific Railway (CPR) steam locomotive (#136), or a 1912 4-6-0 steam locomotive (#1057), hauls a string of 1920s coaches, most painted in the historic CPR maroon. Operations began in 1989, but not before stiff political resistance and nimbyism from the neighbouring township of Innisfil nullified the plan to continue the line beyond Beeton, hence the strangely truncated route.

The trackage constitutes what little remains of the Hamilton and Northwestern Railway, which originally ran between Port Dover, through Hamilton and Allandale, and on to Collingwood and Meaford on Georgian Bay.

When the steam engines are not operating, the coaches are pulled by one of two fifty-year-old diesels. In all, the South Simcoe Railway (SSR) possesses eight coaches and a dozen freight or work cars. Much of the passenger equipment was acquired from the CPR's Credit Valley Railway.

The tiny portable CPR station that once stood in Glen Major serves as the ticket office.

Although the ride is short, the distant column of smoke moving across the farmland and the shriek of the whistle is as genuine a return to the heydays of rail travel as one is likely to get in this province.

THE PORT STANLEY TERMINAL RAILWAY

This 11 kilometre line is part of the famous London and Port Stanley Railway, which began operation in 1856. Not only did it bring tourists to the beaches and resorts of Lake Erie, but also freight for shipment across the lake to Cleveland. Its ownership ended up with the Canadian National Railway, as was the fate of many small early rail operations that closed the section south of St. Thomas in 1982 due to a washout along the line.

This prompted a group of rail enthusiasts and business owners in London to form the Port Stanley Terminal Railway (PSTR). They assembled a fleet of diesel locomotives and passenger coaches and began running excursions from Port Stanley, first to the tiny station at Union. In 1995, excursions were extended to Whytes where the PSTR established a small park. Here, a tank car, snow plough, and caboose are on display

Amongst the rolling stock are six diesel locomotives dating from the 1940s and 1950s, and ten coaches, which date from the 1930s to the 1960s, though the converted caboose goes as far back as 1918. In the yards are a dozen and a half assorted flat cars and cabooses.

The route itself follows the banks of Kettle Creek and offers pastoral views across forests and fields until its destination at Whytes.

With the reinstallation of trackage that the CNR had removed illegally, the tour train will now roll in to the newly constructed replica of the earlier London and Port Stanley Railway station in St. Thomas and on occasion use the Canada Southern station itself.

THE CREDIT VALLEY EXPLORER

The route this tour train follows is arguably southern Ontario's most scenic, as it winds its way down the mighty gorge of the Forks of the Credit Canyon. The route dates back to 1874, when construction began on the Credit Valley Railway (CVR) to connect Toronto with Orangeville and St. Thomas. The line soon became part of the Canadian Pacific Railway (CPR) network. But the CPR also owned the Toronto, Grey and Bruce Railway (TG&B), which largely duplicated the CVR between Toronto and Orangeville, and in the 1930s, the CPR tore up most of the TG&B

south of Orangeville, leaving intact the CVR route through the canyon

By 1990, amid strenuous objections, the CPR had also ripped up the tracks from Orangeville to Owen Sound, selling the remaining line to the Orangeville Rail Development Corporation, which became known as the Orangeville Brampton Railway (OBRY). Although the OBRY railway extends to the CPR's main line in Streetsville, its *Credit Valley Explorer* journeys only to Snelgrove at the north end of Brampton, but offers tourists a spectacular journey unlike any other in southern Ontario.

The popular Credit Valley Explorer gives tourists a stretch in Inglewood.

From a newly built station in Orangeville's historic divisional yards, the tour winds through the hilly farmlands (and golf courses) south from Orangeville before descending into the Forks of the Credit Canyon. The canyon is a defile in the Niagara Escarpment, carved by the Credit River whose two branches tumble together in the canyon's depths.

In its descent, the train passes the ghost town of Cataract Junction, where only rubble remains of a station, hotel, and roundhouse. It then slows to pass another ghostly ruin, that of the Deagle grist mill and power plant, which once provided electricity to Orangeville. The train slows again to cross the high-level, 400-metre trestle above the river's forks, where the views from the coaches are stunning. Making its way out of the canyon, the train passes more rolling farmland (including an Eaton family estate) on to its termination at Snelgrove, a sprawling suburb of Brampton. Light meals are available on board.

THE WATERLOO CENTRAL RAILWAY

When it began operation as the Waterloo and St. Jacobs Railway in 1997, running on a Canadian National Railway (CNR) branch line that linked Kitchener with Elmira, this tour train consisted of what was called a "streamliner" train set. A pair of streamlined diesel locomotives, one at each end, pulled a half-dozen coaches, all painted in the

CNR's elegant green, gold, and black paint scheme. The operation lasted only from 1997 to 2000, when it ceased operations due to maintenance costs.

Meanwhile, in 1993, down in St. Thomas, the Southern Ontario Steam Locomotive Restoration Society was busy restoring the Essex Terminal Railway's steam locomotive #9 to operating condition. When the CNR removed most of the track in and out of St. Thomas the society relocated to Waterloo, and in 2007 was given approval to launch a new tour train, taking #9 with them. There in a new train shed, they incorporated the Waterloo Central Railway, owned by the Region of Waterloo and the City of Waterloo, and began once again to bring #9 up to steam.

But the group also assembled an eclectic collection of a half-dozen coaches, including one built for the CPR in 1928, plus a 1930 baggage car and a 1920 diner car. Their motive power also includes a 70 tonne 1950 diesel locomotive.

After years of restoration, steam once again hauls the Waterloo-St. Jacobs tour train.

Finally, in September 2012, #9 began to puff along the line operating from a replica station in downtown Waterloo to a point north of St. Jacobs, where it crosses a trestle over the Conestoga River, making stops at both St. Jacobs historic village and the renowned St. Jacobs Farmers' Market. Incredibly, those same municipalities are forcing the tour train from its essential downtown Waterloo terminus to a remote suburban location to accommodate a controversial light rail transit line along the tour train's tracks.

THEY CAME AND WENT

Sadly many tour train operations have tried and failed. A short-lived tour train operated between Port Colborne and Welland, but soon ceased operation. Another failed venture was a dinner train between Guelph and Guelph Junction along a former Canadian Pacific Railway (CPR) track owned by the City of Guelph.

But the most noteworthy failure was that of the *Timber Train*. Begun in 1996 along a CPR route known as the Moccasin Line, it ran from Mattawa, located east of North Bay, to Temiscaming in Quebec. Coaches and diesel engines were acquired and painted in the new line's distinctive green and grey paint scheme. In 1998, it won the Ontario's "Best New Attraction" award. But unfortunately that was not to be

its lifeline. Although the narrated seven-hour round-trip included captivating scenery along the banks of the Ottawa River, including a high-level trestle, and although the business community in Temiscaming offered a variety of events in that mill town, it did not translate into passengers, and within a few years the train set was sold to a rail operation in New York state.

The Ontario Northland Railway's popular fall colour train, the *Dreamcatcher Express*, which travelled from North Bay to Temagami over a weekend on late September, perished with Bartelucci's cancellation of the *Northlander*, depriving the business community of Temagami of considerable tourist revenue.

THE REAL DEALS

With Bartolucci's cancellation of the *Northlander*, the only all-purpose rail passenger operations to remain in Ontario were those of the Algoma Central Railway's local train and VIA Rail Canada, and even their schedule was reduced by the Harper government.

VIA's excursions can range from the speedy point-to-point service in the Quebec-Windsor corridor, to more historic routes of the "back line" from Toronto to London, and the *Superior* from Sudbury to White River. The former route follows the original route laid out by the Grand

Trunk in 1856, and stops at or passes by a string of heritage stations in Brampton, Guelph, Kitchener, Stratford, and St. Mary's.

The *Superior* is an all-day trip from Sudbury to White River, and nicknamed (by this author) the "ghost town" train for the many ghost towns, like Nicholson and Lochalsh, through which it passes. It stops at historic communities such as Biscotasing, the one-time home of Grey Owl (real name Archie Belaney[2]), the remote town of Missinaibi, and the busy divisional town of Chapleau, before ending its route in White River, the birth place of a bear cub named "Winnipeg," which became the inspiration for Winnie the Pooh.

VIA Rail's *Canadian* is by far and away the most popular with tourists, and is considered to be one of the world's most beautiful train sets. It was brought into service by the Canadian Pacific Railway (CPR) in 1956 to lure travellers out of their cars and back onto the trains. That didn't work out economically, as today's gridlock will testify. While the portions of the route through southern Ontario occur during the night, the trip through the north explores remote northern communities such as Hornepayne, Armstrong, Nakina, and Sioux Lookout, the latter two towns with their now-restored historic stations. The route also encounters dozens of small First

Passenger coaches languish in a Thunder Bay yard, reflecting the federal government's disinterest in rail passenger service.

Nations communities, as well as scenic lakes and dark tunnels.

VIA's busy and modern Quebec-Windsor Corridor trains rush past much of the scenery along the shores of Lake Ontario and through the rolling farmlands of southwestern Ontario, stopping long enough to see the historic stations at Brantford, Chatham, or Woodstock to the southwest, or Cobourg, Belleville, and Brockville to the east. A few trains may pause at the historic stations in Port Hope, Napanee, or Gananoque Junction.

THE SHORTLINES

Over the years, the major railway companies have employed a dubious policy of dropping their less lucrative branch lines. Even should those lines be earning a modest profit and even should there remain customers who reply upon them, these lines would nonetheless be eliminated.

In many jurisdictions, shortline rail operators would simply purchase the lines and operate them as feeders to the major lines. But in Ontario, prior

VIA Rail Train #1, otherwise known as the westbound Canadian, *takes a break in Hornepayne to allow the train crews to change shifts. The former CN station is clearly showing signs of deterioration.*

to 1996, labour legislation required that shortline operators honour the union contracts already in place. Because the terms of those contracts were more suited to the larger rail operations, they lacked the flexibility that the shortlines needed. An earlier shortline operation, the Goderich and Exeter Railway, for example, was forced to abandon the possible purchase of a CN branch line from Stratford to Owen Sound for that reason.

But that all changed in 1996 when the Ontario government amended the labour laws to remove railway union successor rights. Almost overnight, shortlines moved in to save many branch lines from removal. While labour unions decried the change, shortlines today provide jobs for more than 400 rail employees, jobs which would have otherwise been scrapped along with the branch lines.[3]

ESSEX TERMINAL RAILWAY

Well before the labour laws were first changed in the early 1990s there was the Essex Terminal Railway (ETR), one of Ontario's oldest shortlines, dating to 1902. It was originally chartered to link the then-Grand Trunk with the Canadian Bridge plant in Windsor. By 1918, the line extended down the Detroit River to a location called Quarries, in today's Amherstburg. Although tracks no longer run to Amherstburg, the shortline, now run by Essex Moterm Holdings Ltd., continues to serve industries in the Windsor and Lasalle areas. Its historic ETR steam locomotive, #9, now resides in St. Jacobs, where the Southern Ontario Steam Locomotive Restoration Society has restored it to running condition.

THE GODERICH AND EXETER RAILWAY

This American-owned company began running its trains over the former CN lines from Goderich to London and from Clinton to Centralia, a total of 120 kilometres. By 1998, it had leased trackage from CN from Georgetown to London and was soon serving communities such as St. Mary's, Guelph, Cambridge, and Kitchener-Waterloo. Its twelve diesel engines (some dating to the 1950s) were hauling 25,000 carloads each year, containing salt, fertilizer, wheat, soy meal, and auto parts.

ONTARIO SOUTHLAND RAILWAY

The Ontario Southland Railway (OSR) is another extensive shortline operator that today operates on trackage between Ingersoll and Tillsonburg, Woodstock and St. Thomas, and Guelph and Campbellville. It owns more than 120 kilometres of tracks and benefits more than two-dozen customers. It began operations in 1992 and is Canadian-owned.

TRILLIUM RAILWAY

This southwestern Ontario line started up in 1997 and operates two lines, that linking St. Thomas with Delhi, and the Port Colborne Harbour Railway. Two dozen customers line the 100 kilometres of tracks.

SOUTHERN ONTARIO RAILWAY

This shortline was set up to serve a new industrial area on the shores of Lake Erie, a complex known as Nanticoke, named after an earlier fishing village. Operated by Rail America and based in Hamilton, the 85-kilometre line hauls 44,000 carloads per year, including steel, fuel, and chemicals for Nanticoke, as well industries in Caledonia, which include gypsum and kitty litter.

THE ORANGEVILLE BRAMPTON RAILWAY

This is Ontario's only shortline to carry passengers as well as freight. While the *Credit Valley Explorer* is described under tour trains, the Orangeville Brampton Railway (OBRY), which took over 55 kilometres of the Canadian Pacific Railway's abandoned Owen Sound subdivision, carries freight from Orangeville south to Streetsville, where it connects with the CPR. Operating two days a week, the OBRY hauls product from the half-dozen members of the Orangeville-Brampton Rail Access Group, which maintains the track, while Cando Contracting operates the trains themselves.

THE BARRIE-COLLINGWOOD RAILWAY

While this shortline is also operated by Cando, its success was short-lived. In 2011, the town of Collingwood, worried over expenditures, offered for sale the section between Utopia, the headquarters for the line, and Collingwood, a distance of 34 kilometres. The operation began in 1998 with two diesel locomotives. As of 2012, the Barrie-Collingwood Railway still serves industries in the Barrie area.

ONTARIO L'ORIGNAL RAILWAY

Although the former Hawkesbury branch of the CNR was put up for sale in 1996, it has returned to the company's fold. Between 1996 and 2001, Rail America ran the line as the Ontario L'Orignal Railway, serving the communities of Hawkesbury, L'Orignal, and Dalkeith, linking with the CN at Glen Robertson. In 2001, the Ottawa Central Railway purchased the operation and ran it until 2008, when the CN once again assumed the line. Its main customer continues to be the Ivaco Rolling Mills in L'Orignal.

ONTARIO'S TOP TRAIN-WATCHING SPOTS

This author's fondest childhood memories are those of travelling to the Canadian Pacific Railway's Leaside station to watch the steam engines hauling the freight trains through the area. Many train enthusiasts have carried this love into adulthood and gather at some of Ontario's most heavily travelled rail routes to photograph or record the freight and passenger trains.

One of the most favoured sites is a footbridge in the Laking Garden of the Royal Botanical Gardens in Burlington. This location offers an unimpeded view of Bayview Junction. It is here that the busy tracks from Toronto branch off with the western link, continuing westerly to London and Windsor, and the southerly route makes its way to Hamilton and Niagara Falls. Train spotters are treated not only to the many Canadian National (CN) and Canadian Pacific (CPR) freights that

Some of Ontario's most popular train-spotting takes place on the Newtonville Road bridge, where VIA, CN, and CP action can be seen.

rumble through, but also VIA Rail, Amtrak, and GO trains.

East of Toronto, the main lines of the CNR and CPR come within a few metres of each other and lure rail train lovers to the overpasses, which offer views of trains approaching through the rolling farmlands. A favourite is the bridge on Newtonville Road, where vehicular traffic is light.

Only a few kilometres east of that point is the Port Hope waterfront. A pair of massive trestles here carries the main lines of both the CPR and the CNR over the Ganaraska River where as many as fourteen trains, both freight and passenger, may cross within an hour. To add to the appeal, VIA Rail's historic 1857 Grand Trunk station lies only a few metres away, where four VIA trains stop each day.

The historic Memory Junction Railway Museum in Brighton not only has the benefit of the CNR and CPR lines adjacent to each other, but also that of an 1857 Grand Trunk (GT) station and steam train display. Similarly, the GT station in Cobourg not only offers the same main line opportunities, but also the many VIA Rail train stops and a comfortable waiting room.

The busy CPR yards at Smiths Falls offer frequent CPR freight movements, as well as several Toronto to Ottawa VIA trains each day. Happily, the large former-CPR station still stands, although VIA now stops at a new shelter at the north end of the town. An added benefit is the large railway museum at the west end of the town.

Train watchers will also gather at the magnificent GT station in Brantford to observe VIA and CN rail activity, and then retire to the café situated in the former baggage room.

— 10 —
THE RAIL TRAILS

In a sadly ironic twist, Ontario enjoys some of the most extensive and scenic of Canada's rail trails, regrettably owing to the demise, often unnecessarily, of much of the province's once-extensive network of rail lines.

The major flurry of line abandonment didn't start until the 1980s. Local industries were switching to trucks and "just in time" delivery. Within two decades, more than half of Ontario's tracks had vanished. While many of the rights of way were simply turned over to adjacent property owners, others went on to become some of the province's more popular and scenic rail trails, and in that capacity help to celebrate Ontario's railway heritage.

THE ELORA-CATARACT TRAIL

When the Credit Valley Railway was built from Toronto to Orangeville in 1881, it extended a branch line from Cataract Junction deep in the Forks of the Credit Canyon to Elora. While the line to Orangeville remains part of the Orangeville Brampton Railway, popular for its tour train excursions, the branch to Elora is now the 47-kilometre Elora-Cataract Rail Trail. The route rises out of the deep gorge to cross farmland and pass through a variety of historic villages such as Erin, Hillsburg, and Fergus, before ending in Elora. Little of railway vintage remains along this route, save for a high bridge over the Grand River between Fergus and Elora.

THE FRIENDSHIP TRAIL

This well-groomed and popular trail follows the route of the Buffalo, Brantford and Goderich Railway between Fort Erie and Port Colborne. Being rather flat and straight, the trail offers little in the way of scenery and railway heritage. Port Colborne does still have its CNR station, which now houses a restaurant and the offices of the Trillium Railway.

THE BRANTFORD TRAILS

Although Brantford never developed as a major rail hub like Stratford, it has become a hub for many of Ontario's rail trails. The 32-kilometre Hamilton to Brantford Rail Trail follows the abandoned portion of the Toronto, Hamilton and Buffalo Railway (TH&B) from the west end of Hamilton to downtown Brantford. Its effective trail head, however, lies in the Dundas Valley Conservation Area at a replica station with historic railway rolling stock. In Brantford the trail stops short of the historic TH&B station in downtown Brantford.

From Brantford, the Lake Erie and Northern rail trail, known locally as the S.C. Johnson Trail, follows the scenic banks of the Grand River north through Paris, and then for 19 kilometres on the Cambridge to Paris Rail Trail to the south end of Galt. En route it passes beneath the Grand Trunk trestle over the river and offers a scenic lookout from the ruins of the Great Western Bridge, a short distance north.

From Brantford, two rail trails lead south, one that follows the TH&B, here known as the Gordon Graves Memorial Parkway, and the other the Lake Erie and Northern (LE&N), until the two meet in Mount Pleasant. Then the trail follows the TH&B south into Waterford, where it ends. Here the LE&N takes over again, encountering the high-level bridge (not yet upgraded to be part of the trail), and the early Michigan Central station.

From Waterford, the Waterford Heritage Trail follows the LE&N to Simcoe where it then links with the Lynn Valley Trail for its final leg into the north end of Port Dover.

RAIL TRAILS IN GREY AND BRUCE

Several rail trails follow the early rail lines in this area, making for a pleasant trail system.

The roadbed of the former Stratford and Huron (S&H) line has been developed as a trail leading from Britton into Listowel, where it passes the former Grand Trunk station, now converted to a Kinsman meeting hall. From Listowel, a rail trail follows the route of the Wellington, Grey and Bruce (WG&B) southward through Atwood and Brussels, before ending in the hamlet of Henfryn.

In Hanover, where the Canadian Pacific Railway (CPR) and the Stratford and Huron lines intersected, the two rights-of-way have combined to form a local walking trail, portions of which use the old railway bridges over the Saugeen River.

A short trail follows the Stratford and Huron (S&H) through Chesley, soaring over the high-level trestle above the Saugeen, and is known here as the Chesley Heritage Trail. Further north, the scenic Keppel Rail Trail follows the Owen Sound branch of the S&H from Park Head down the Niagara Escarpment and into Owen Sound, where it ends at the historic CN station, now a museum. On the opposite side of the harbour, the Tom Thomson Trail follows a portion of the Toronto, Grey and Bruce (TG&B) along the water from a point just north of the vacant CPR station.

In 1872, the Wellington, Grey and Bruce railway began to establish a network of lines through the Grey and Bruce area. Branches led variously to Southampton, Kincardine, Palmerston, Guelph, and Elora. An intermittent rail trail links Palmerston, once a key rail hub, with Southampton. From Palmerston to Walkerton, the trail passes a pair of early trestles as well as the Grand Trunk (GT) station still in place in Harriston. North of Walkerton it becomes the Bruce Rail Trail. In Paisley, it encounters a pair of light-level trestles over the Saugeen River before making its way into Southampton, although it stops well short of the historic brick GT station there.

The WG&B branch that leads to Kincardine

has been developed into a short trail through Wingham, where it crosses the high-level bridge over the Maitland River and encounters the restored GT station. In Kincardine, a nature trail follows the old roadbed along the Lake Huron beach.

THE KISSING BRIDGE TRAIL

Following the route of the Guelph and Goderich Railway, a Canadian Pacific Railway (CPR) line that opened after years of delay in 1907, this trail is inconsistently maintained, in places blocked by adjacent landowners. The better portions are those from Guelph to Linwood and from Auburn to Goderich. The remainder are crude ATV trails, or barely visible at all.

The piers of the CPR bridge over the Grand River remain visible, while in Blyth, the Blyth Greenway Trail passes a rare water tower, which has been retained. Between Auburn and Goderich it becomes the Auburn-Goderich and the Tiger Dunlop Trails. At Goderich, it crosses the historic Menesetung Bridge over the Maitland River and ends near the impressive Goderich CPR station.

ST. MARY'S "GRAND TRUNK TRAIL"

This short 2.8-kilometre route follows the original right-of-way of the Grand Trunk Railway through the north end of St. Mary's. From the GT's historic 1858 stone station, the trail strikes through the community before crossing the impressive "Sarnia Bridge" over the Thames River.

SARNIA, THE HOWARD WATSON TRAIL

While much of the Grand Trunk west of St. Mary's has gone to private hands, the westernmost 16-kilometre segment from Camlachie to east end Sarnia is now the Howard Watson Trail. The trail is well groomed for cyclists and hikers, passes farms and suburban developments, and is close enough to the shores of Lake St. Clair for users to spend time on a sandy beach.

CHRYSLER CANADA GREENWAY

Following the route of Hiram Walker's Lake Erie and Detroit River Railway, this well-groomed trail extends from a point south of Windsor near Oldcastle, and ends near Leamington at Colasanti's Tropical Gardens. The 42-kilometre route is maintained by the Essex Region Conservation Authority and is named in appreciation of the large donation by Chrysler Canada to help acquire the line in 1995. Use of the trail is for hikers and cyclists, as well as cross-country skiers. Horses are permitted on a few portions. Washrooms are at the trail's two termini

and picnic tables are plentiful. The trail's most significant heritage feature is the restored stone station in Kingsville, a rare example of a Richardsonian Romanesque architectural style.

The preserved Kingsville Station is now a restaurant on the Chrysler Canada Greenway rail trail.

THE CALEDON TRAILWAY

The origin of this scenic 36-kilometre trail lies with the Hamilton and Lake Erie Railway and the Hamilton and Northwestern Railway, which in 1877 completed a link from Port Dover on Lake Erie to Collingwood on Georgian Bay. The Caledon Trailway begins in Terra Cotta and follows the Credit River past the historic ruins of the Cheltenham Brickworks and the village of Cheltenham itself, with its classic stone general store.

At Inglewood it crosses the active tracks of the Orangeville Brampton Railway, before encountering the spectacular scenery of the Niagara Escarpment. At the crossing between the two lines are nestled the foundations of the Inglewood station, and across the tracks a general store now occupies the former railway hotel. The rights-of-way through the villages of Caledon East and Palgrave have been attractively landscaped, while a pair of shelters waits in Inglewood and Palgrave. The trail terminates near the gates of the South Simcoe Steam Railway.

THE GEORGIAN TRAIL

This popular 36-kilometre rail trail picks up the Hamilton and Northwestern (H&NW) from Brick Street in Collingwood, and follows the shores of Georgian Bay to the harbour at Meaford. En route, the trail passes the historic Craigleith station. With its decorative tower, the building, after several decades as a restaurant, is now the Craigleith Heritage Museum. At Thornbury the trail crosses a historic wooden trestle over the Beaver River and ends near the former H&NW freight shed on Meaford harbour.

THE NORTH SIMCOE AND TINY RAIL TRAIL

Chartered as the North Simcoe Railway in 1878, this route was intended to link the H&NW with Penetanguishene on Georgian Bay. Following CN's abandonment in 1991, the portion between Sunnidale and Penetang has become the North Simcoe Trail as far as Elmvale, where it becomes the Tiny Rail Trail to Midland and Penetang, a combined 55 kilometres. While no railway structures have survived, the route does offer vistas across the Minesing Swamp and access to the fading ghosts of the sawmill village of Josephine. A replica station serves as a trail shelter in the village of Perkinsfield.

THE UHTOFF TRAIL

This 28-kilometre trail follows the route of the Canadian Pacific Railway northwesterly from the Orillia waterfront into Coldwater. From the waterfront location, the short Lightfoot Memorial Trail leads southeasterly to the site of the Stephen Leacock Museum and the Grand Trunk swing bridge over the Atherley Narrows, which divides Lake Couchiching from Lake Simcoe

THE TAY SHORE TRAIL

Another of the more scenic rail trails, this route follows the 1879 route of the Midland Railway from Waubaushene to Midland, where it becomes the Midland Rotary Trail. Much of the 24 kilometres follows the shore of Georgian Bay, offering scenic vistas across the waters. The trail is paved and passes various amenities such as benches and information plaques, one of which describes the Hogg Bay Trestle, which before it was removed in 1978, was Ontario's longest wooden trestle. Entering Midland, the trail crosses the Wye River on a wooden trestle located beside the recreated Sainte-Marie Among the Hurons mission.

The Tay Shore rail trail includes historical plaques such as this, which tells of the Hogg Bay trestle that once stood here.

THE TORONTO BELT LINE

The Toronto Belt Line was a commuter railway that was more than a century ahead of its time. Incorporated in 1889 to offer a loop through what was intended to be an area of suburban growth north of the then-city limits, the projected growth stagnated and the rail line closed. Service ended in 1890, and portions were assumed by the Grand Trunk, some of which continued to serve the CN until 1988. Today, it has become one of Toronto's more popular urban trailways known variously as the Kay Gardner Beltline Park and the York Beltline Trail. The eastern end of the route begins by Evergreen Brickworks in the Don Valley, and follows a forested ravine as far as Mount Pleasant Cemetery. It resumes near Yonge Street, crossing on an historic steel girder bridge, and ends at the Allen Road. The York Beltline Trail begins at Marlee and follows a mostly urban landscape.

THE GUELPH RADIAL TRAIL

Inaugurated by the Canadian Northern Railway in 1911, the Toronto and Suburban Railway (T&S) was, like all of Ontario's electric radial lines, fated to be short-lived. Competition and conniving by the car, oil, and tire industries saw most of the lines gone by the 1930s. The T&S carried streetcars from Toronto to Guelph, but was abandoned in 1935.

A small section forms part of the Halton County Radial Railway and Streetcar Museum near Rockwood, while the western-most 28 kilometres has become the Guelph Radial Trail, portions of which are well groomed for hiking and cycling, while other portions are little more than a rough trail. Although the original Meadowvale shelter now sits on the right-of-way in the museum grounds, no other heritage features have survived.

THE GRAND JUNCTION/TRANS CANADA TRAIL

This hit-and-miss trail follows the route of what began as the Grand Junction Railway, intended to loop north from Belleville through Lindsay before returning to Lake Ontario, likely near Port Hope. The tracks made it to Peterborough where they became part of the Grand Trunk's expanding empire.

The trail begins at Corbyville, an abandoned distillery town north of Belleville, and winds its way northwesterly through farmlands. The most historic sight on the route is the preserved and historic Stirling station. Upgraded by the municipality, the historical society, and the Rotary club, this two-storey Van Horne-style station has become a museum and community meeting hall.

The trail continues through the pastoral countryside, interrupted by the Trent Canal at Campellford and Hastings. After winding through the scenic Peterborough drumlin fields, the newly opened trail ends near Peterborough.

THE TRAILS OF THE TRENT

Between Peterborough and the town of Lakefield, the former roadbed of the Midland Railway, later the Grand Trunk, is now the Rotary Greenway Trail and the Lakefield Rail Trail. Interrupted by the grounds of Trent University, the trail follows close to the scenic banks of the Trent River before ending at the historic wooden Grand Trunk station in Lakefield, which is now a used book store.

THE MIDLAND TRAIL

Prior to the growth of the Grand Trunk, the Midland Railway, based in Port Hope, was one of Ontario's more aggressive rail lines, acquiring many of the smaller lines before its own amalgamation with the GT in 1888. From downtown Peterborough, near the historic Hutchinson House, the trail trends westward towards the former rail hub of Lindsay. A short distance west of Peterborough the trail crosses the dizzying Double Trestle, a nine-span iron trestle spanning 200-meters long and rising high above Buttermilk Creek. A much lower wooden trestle carries it across the Pigeon River in Omemee.

THE KAWARTHA TRANS CANADA TRAIL

In Lindsay, the Midland Railway, while no longer a trail west of the town, does link with two other rail trails. In 1876, the tracks of the Whitby and Port Perry Railway were extended into Lindsay. Today, that right of way is a groomed trail between Lindsay and Cresswell, and is known as the Kawartha Trans Canada Trail. At Blackwater Junction, once a busy rail stop, it connects with the Beaver Meadow Wetland Trail, part of the former Toronto and Nipissing Railway that leads to Uxbridge. For the most part, the trails pass through pastoral farmlands, where the only railway structures are the former freight shed at Mariposa and the historic Grand Trunk "witch's hat" station in Uxbridge, now a terminus for the York and Durham Heritage Railway.

THE VICTORIA
AND THE HALIBURTON RAIL TRAILS

The other Lindsay rail link was that with the former route of the Victoria Railway. Started in 1874, the line leads north from Lindsay to the town of Haliburton. This resource line hauled mostly lumber and tourists bound for Haliburton's scenic lakelands in the summer. Passenger service ended in the 1960s and all rail traffic in the 1980s. The railway heritage abounds along this 90-kilometre route, where historic stations yet stand in Fenelon Falls, Kinmount, and Haliburton. A one-time hand-operated turntable pit remains at Howland Junction, while historic bridges remain at Fenelon Falls, with a swing bridge over the Trent-Severn Waterway at Burnt River, Howland, and near the ghost town of Gelert. The ghostly shells of the Standard Chemical plant, built in 1900, lurk in the woods beside the trail at Donald.

THE K&P TRAIL

The Kingston and Pembroke Railway (K&P) was affectionately know as the "Kick and Push" for the many hills around it, which its engines had to huff and puff. This resource line hauled primarily lumber, and iron ore from the little mines that lined the route. The Canadian Pacific Railway (CPR) began lifting the rails in 1962 and completed the job in 1986. Most of the route from Renfrew (it never did reach Pembroke) has become a rail trail in varying states of maintenance. While some parts are ideal for hiking and cycling, especially near Kingston, others are the purview of lumber trucks and ATVs. Although the only station to linger is that at Clarendon Station, a long causeway marks the route across scenic Calabogie Lake. A railway display at Sharbot Lake marks the junction of the Kingston and Pembroke Railway with the Ontario and Quebec Railway, and includes a caboose and a kiosk displaying the history of the station that stood there. Small ghost towns appear at the former iron mining locations of Robertsville and Wilbur, while still-active communities like Lavant Station and Snow Road Station retain a variety of heritage homes and churches.

THE CENTRAL ONTARIO RAILWAY

The vestiges of this long resource line now form the Prince Edward County Trail, the Lower Trent

Trail, and the Hastings Heritage Trail. The section from Picton to Trenton began as the Prince Edward County Railway in 1873, before joining the Central Railway in 1881. The route then took it through Trenton and up the centre of Hastings County to Bancroft and Maynooth. For the most part, the trains hauled lumber and minerals from the many little mines in the Coe Hill and Bancroft areas. One of its biggest customers was the Marmoraton Iron Mine at Marmora. Now abandoned, its massive open pit is slowly filling with water.

While the Prince Edward County portion is well groomed for hiking and cycling, the more northerly portions in Hastings are more suited for ATVs and snowmobiles. On the Prince Edward portion, a freight shed and feed mill survive by the trail in Consecon, while Picton's two early stations have found new uses. Central Ontario Railway stations still stand in Bancroft and Maynooth, as does the former Hogans railway hotel in Millbridge Station, which is now a ghost town. The once-booming gold town of Eldorado is similarly a ghost town as well, with a number of old buildings that date back to the boom times when the place was the centre of Ontario's first gold rush.

THE CATARAQUI TRAIL

In 1911, the dynamic railway duo of Mackenzie and Mann completed the Canadian Northern Railway (CNo) from Toronto to Ottawa. But by the 1930s the line, then part of the Canadian National Railway (CNR), was duplicating that company's other lines, and the route was gradually abandoned. The portion that still stretches from Strathcona, north of Napanee, to Smiths Falls now forms the 184-kilometre Cataraqui Trail. Although portions are sufficiently rough to make it unrideable for cyclists, the more scenic section between Chaffeys Locks and Sydenham is better kept and has become popular with hikers and cyclists. Here it winds though the granite hills of the Canadian Shield and along the shores of Sydenham Lake. While no stations remain along the trail, a few heritage railway bridges remain, such as that over the Rideau Canal at Chaffey's Locks and over the Napanee River at Yarker.

THE OTTAWA CARLETON TRAILWAY

This 32-kilometre groomed rail trail traces the route of the Canadian Pacific Railway (CPR) line between Carleton Place and Ottawa. After the tracks were lifted in 1990, the portion between the CPR bridge at Robertson Road, west of Ottawa, and the eastern outskirts of Carleton Place, became a rail trail. Although most of the trail passes level farm fields, a replica water tower, which serves as a children's apparatus, and station-like trail shelter and washroom have been added in downtown Stittsville.

The trail ends close to the historic CPR station in Carleton Place

NORTHERN SNOWMOBILE TRAILS

Although generally unsuited for cyclists and all but the hardier hikers, the snowmobile rail trails have at least helped celebrate the province's railway heritage. The former Booth Line, which originally led from Ottawa to Georgian Bay, is now a popular snowmobile trail from the vicinity of Highway 11 to Highway 400, known as the Seguin Trail. Here it passes through forests, and crosses small rivers and creeks and pioneer towns like Orrville and Spence, as well as ghost towns like Seguin Falls and Swords. West of Highway 400, it continues as the Rose Point Trail to the swing bridge leading to Parry Island. East of Algonquin Park from Whitney to near Eganville it is similarly a snowmobile trail, while a

The Ottawa Carleton rail trail shows some imagination with playground equipment as it resembles a railway water tower and a "station" washroom.

few sections within the park are now popular hiking routes. Along the way it encounters the Polish heritage centre in Wilno, and the covered former railway bridge over Brennan's Creek in Killaloe.

The former roadbed of the Canadian Pacific Railway's Ontario and Quebec Railway has similarly become a lengthy snowmobile and ATV trail that winds through the rocklands from east of Havelock to near Glen Tay. Unfortunately, nothing of heritage interest lingers along this route. As of 2012, however, plans are afoot to re-lay the tracks from Havelock to Norwood to accommodate a proposed Toronto commuter rail service to be known as the Shining Waters Railway.

— 11 —

THE WRITING ON THE WALLS:
ONTARIO'S RAILWAY MURALS

It began in Chemainus, British Columbia, when a town council, trying to avoid becoming a ghost town when its mill closed, decided to try to lure tourists by engaging the country's top mural artists to depict the town's history on the sides of its buildings. The high-quality and evocative imagery quickly turned the dying community into one of Vancouver Island's tourist destinations.

The idea began to spread across the country, with Athens, Ontario, being the first in the province to muralize its main street. Today, more than one hundred towns and villages around Ontario have adopted the technique, some content with but a mural or two while others have created and promoted an outdoor gallery of historic murals, many of which depict the town's railway heritage.

Regrettably, one difficulty lies in how to maintain the murals once they start to fade, especially in cases where the original artist is no longer available.

It is indeed sad that the more than thirty of the fine murals of Athens, the town that introduced outdoor murals to Ontario, have so badly deteriorated that several are barely visible, including the 1986 mural by Laurie Maruczak entitled *Train Station*, which depicts the arrival of a Brockville and Westport steam locomotive at the town's first station. It remains, for now, at the northeast corner of Henry and Main Street.

Chatham's *All Aboard*, painted by C. Penelope Duschene in 2003, portrays an old wood-burning steam engine in front of the town's Richardsonian Canadian Pacific Railway (CPR) station, which is now a garden centre east of the city. The 16-by-60 foot mural rests on the wall of the former Dover Flour Mills at Colborne and William Streets.

A mural depicting various facets of Ingersoll's heritage sits on Highway 19 north of the 401, and includes the Grand Trunk station, which sadly lies vacant, vandalized, and neglected.

At the corner of West Street and Court House Square in Goderich, a small mural of the Goderich CPR station, which still stands close to the harbour, can be found.

Individual murals in both Wingham and Shallow Lake show train time at the respective stations. While the building depicted in Shallow Lake is no longer there, that in Wingham has been carefully restored.

A series of four images at the corner of Inkerman and Queen Street in historic Paisley include the arrival of a Canadian National Railway (CNR) train at the village station.

On the north side of Hamilton's Main Street, between James and Hughson, a large mural includes an early steam train among the various images of days gone by.

In Collingwood, a ski train is shown arriving at the little Craigleith station situated at the foot of the Blue Mountain ski hills. The station still stands and is now a museum. The mural is at the corner of Simcoe and Hurontario Streets.

Arguably Ontario's best collection of outdoor murals is that of more than three-dozen in Midland, most painted by Fred Lenz before he passed away while working on his last project. Two images illustrate the Midland Railway, one showing a train at the early station, while another is of the roundhouse.

The towns that grew along the tracks of the Toronto, Grey and Bruce Railway have an affinity for depicting their train stations. Such murals appear in Dundalk, Markdale, and Shelburne. In Dundalk, the wall of the *Dundalk Herald* vividly depicts an early CPR steam locomotive arriving at the station. Tracks and station are both gone. Not far from Dundalk, a large mural in Markdale similarly depicts a 1940s-era image of train time at that town's CPR station. It is on the corner of Toronto Street and Main Street. The trend also repeats in Shelburne, to the south of these two towns, where a mural at the intersection of Main and Victoria Streets shows train time at the last Shelburne station. That building is now a private home south of the town.

A painting on the side of a Broadway Avenue store in Orangeville shows a CPR steam train arriving at the CPR station, originally on the Toronto, Grey and Bruce line. That station is now a restaurant, while its original site now contains a more modern station for tourists riding the Credit Valley Explorer.

The old and new versions of Sarnia's historic St. Clair tunnel appear on the side of a building at Front Street near Cromwell.

It should come as no surprise that a town that bills itself as the "Railway City," St. Thomas would offer up nearly half of its thirteen murals with railway themes. *Memories of the Marquette Yards* was created by Fred Harrison and lies on Elgin Street, *Foundation of Town and Rail* on Hincks Street was created by Paul Membourquette, while renowned muralists Dan Sawatzky, who created many of Chemainus's finest murals, and his brother Peter put their paints to work with *The Canada Southern* on New Street and the rather dreamy *When I'm*

Big, a 30 by 50 foot work on the northeast corner of Talbot and Flora Streets that shows a young boy clearly dreaming of growing up to work on the railway.

The tracks of the London and Port Stanley Railway once linked St. Thomas with Port Stanley on Lake Erie, and so it was that group of artists, headed by Candy McManiman, created a mural in Port Stanley showing the town's station as it appeared in 1896. A newer station is headquarters for the Port Stanley Terminal Railway tour trains.

St. Thomas offers several rail-themed outdoor murals, including When I'm Big *by accomplished muralist Dan Sawatzky.*

Another community famous for its murals is Welland. Among the three-dozen images that depict the heritage of this canal town is *Tell Me About the Old Time Trains* overlooking a Main Street parking lot. It is yet another of Dan Sawatzky's wonderful creations.

The suburbs of Scarborough are an unlikely place to find murals, especially one about the area's railway heritage. But on the side of a Kingston Road store near the corner of St. Clair Avenue East and Kingston Road, a large mural by Phil Jennifer and Jamie Richards named *In the Way of Progress* depicts a recumbent cow impeding the progress of an interurban streetcar which, until the 1930s, provided public transit on Kingston Road.

A fine mural entitled *Orono Early 1900s* shows the Canadian Northern's Orono railway station, a building and rail line, both of which have been gone since the 1940s. The street that replaced the tracks goes by the name Station Road.

Although tracks and station have long gone, a mural in the town of Milbrook offers a view of train time at its old station.

On the side of the Grand Trunk (GT) station in Brockville, now a VIA Rail station, a large mural depicts the 1951 visit to the town by Princess Elizabeth and the Duke of Edinborough. However, in the mural the Maple Leaf flag, which flutters above the station, did not arrive until more than a decade later.

In Morrisburg, *World War Two Homecoming* shows soldiers returning to the town's original Grand Trunk stone station on a CNR train, with its green and gold paint scheme. The mural is on the side of the Giant Tiger store, close to where the station once stood before being removed to make way for the flooding from the St. Lawrence Seaway. The mural was created by David Yentman in 2003.

Pembroke is another community that has embraced outdoor murals to celebrate its heritage. Beginning with five murals in 1990, the town's outdoor gallery has grown to thirty-three murals, which collectively depict the historical development of the community. Action at Pembroke's long-gone Union Station is shown in a mural at Pembroke and Alexander Streets. It was created by Robin Burgess in 1996. The historic CPR water tower sports a wraparound mural that depicts the old Pembroke sawmill.

Another prominent muralist, Allen Hillgendorf, created railway images for both Killaloe and Wilberforce. That in Killaloe, on the town's post office, depicts train time at the old Booth-style station, while that in Wilberforce shows soldiers returning from war to the boxcar-sized station in the village. In both places tracks and stations are long gone.

In Gravenhurst, a wonderfully executed mural by Andrew Mill shows Gravenhurst's first station, built by the Northern and Northwest Railway. The station building was replaced, by the Grand

Trunk, with the delightful wooden station that survives today. Trains once again show up in Cam Lane's mural at the corner of Sharpe Street and Muskoka Road, as they wait at Muskoka Wharf station where the steamers *Segwun* and *Sagamo* have just disembarked their passengers.

MacTier began as a CPR divisional town called Muskoka Station. It still remains a busy CPR point and to help celebrate that heritage,

the Foodland store shows the CPR's 1939 Royal Tour train stopped at the MacTier station. The station depicted in that image has been replicated to become the town's new library.

In the northwestern Ontario town of Keewatin, a pair of murals are featured on the walls of the museum. On the east wall, a mural entitled *Romance of the Railway* shows a variety of railway scenes over the years, including building the

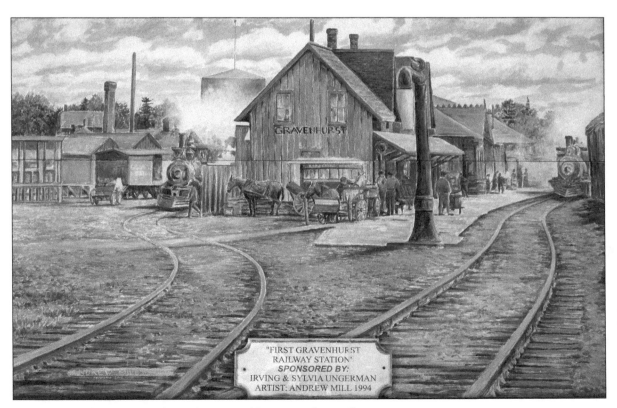

The first Gravenhurst station is depicted on a mural by artist Andrew Mill.

line, and the arrival of the Princess of Dufferin, the CPR's first transcontinental steam engine. On the west wall a second mural depicts the 1939 Royal Tour, the CPR's *Canadian*, and an image of a modern container train. The murals are the creation of Don Makela, who completed them in 2003. The *Power of Vision* by Joseph Cross, on the side of Bigway Foods, depicts among other images the arrival of the CPR's "Campers Special" at the one-time Keewatin station.

In the adjacent town of Kenora, a CPR divisional town, a series of panels on the side of the Kenora Telephone building by British Columbia's Mike Svob, done in 1995, depict railway days in the town, including a steam train and the station, which still serves the CPR.

And it would be only natural, since Ignace owes its existence to having been a CPR divisional town, for it to have a mural of its old station. Although trains still pass, the CPR removed the designated station in recent times. The mural is at Main and Rand Streets.

In Nipigon, a fine mural entitled *Racing the Train* is slowly fading away on the side of a building

Racing the Train, *a Dan Sawatzky mural, is fading from the side of this Nipigon building.*

on Railway Street. It depicts a determined dog dashing across the tracks as a steam train pulls up to the old Nipigon station. The CPR demolished the station in 1988, ignoring a determined fundraising effort by the residents to save it. Hopefully, a bit of that determination will save the 1999 mural, especially as it was done by renowned mural artist, Dan Sawatzky.

White River is a divisional town established by the CPR, so it is fitting that the museum should display a trio of murals that depict the White River stations, the original and the current. An even more significant portrayal is that of the childrens' favourite literary character, White River's own Winnie the Pooh, covered in the chapter on towns.

The divisional CPR town of Chapleau boasts of its rail roots in a main street mural that combines a diesel, a steam locomotive, and the CPR corporate logo in a single image.

THE OTHER LAST SPIKE

But murals do not represent the only way in which the railway heritage of Ontario is depicted in visual form.

There is the cairn dedicated to the CPR's "other" last spike. While the completion of the CPR's transcontinental route was widely celebrated by the driving of the "Last Spike" by CPR president Donald Smith at Craigellachie on November 7, 1885, and widely popularized in the famous photo by Alexander Ross, another "last spike" was pounded into the tracks six months earlier. It was on the shores of Lake Superior, at Noslo, west of the port of Jackfish, that the CPR drove the last spike to represent the completion of the Lake Superior portion of the line. And, as at Craigellachie, a cairn also marks the spot.

But it wasn't until fifty years after the event that war veterans and former CPR employees who originally participated, gathered to inaugurate a memorial cairn. The attractive monument, which rests on a base of local stones, has inscribed in local rock the words: "Driving the last spike between Montreal and Winnipeg was re-enacted here by veterans and some original participants on May 16, 1935. This monument was erected on this spot to commemorate this historical occasion."

THE MYSTERY CARVINGS

A somewhat less formal monument is etched on the side of a railway rock cut south of Gravenhurst. The unusually flat surface proved ideal for a group of railway surveyors and later workmen to carve their names. Here, etched in the granite, in letters as high as four inches, some in gothic script, others in Arabic, are fifty-five initials or names, the oldest that of J. Gibbs, carved in 1875. Others were added in the late 1870s, the most recent in 1925.

Early rail workers and surveyors have left a historic imprint on a rock-cut near Gravenhurst.

Although darkened by a century and a half of passing trains, the slight overhang has helped to protect this remarkable piece of Ontario's railway heritage from the elements. An ancient wooden survey stake sits in the ground beside the overhang.[1]

NOTES

INTRODUCTION

1. R.L. Kennedy, articles in "Old Time Trains," *www.trainweb.org.*

2. As Transport Minister to the Pearson government, Jack Pickersgill claimed passenger trains to be obsolete and that they belonged only in museums, an attitude that has not entirely dissipated within the ranks of the Harper government of 2013.

CHAPTER 1

1. Jane Pitfield, *Leaside* (Toronto: Natural Heritage Books, 1999) 22–38. This chapter outlines the rise of Leaside with the Canadian Northern Railway's York Land Company, which laid out the community in 1912.

2. According to the *Canadian Encyclopaedia*, nephaline syenite is an igneous rock composed of nephaline, soda, and potash feldspar and is used in the making of glass and ceramics. Operations began at an open pit mine at Blue Mountain, north of Havelock, in 1932 and continue to this day. The raw material is shipped by rail through Havelock.

3. The 350-foot S.S. *Keewatin* steamship was launched in 1907 at the Fairfield Shipbuilding Docks in Scotland and joined a fleet of five CPR steamships that conducted passenger cruises

from primarily Port McNicoll to Port Arthur for six decades. The *Keewatin* was retired in 1965, destined for the scrapyard until it was rescued by R.J. Peterson of Douglas, Michigan, who towed it to the mouth of the Kalamazoo River on Lake Michigan, where it operated for forty-five years as a floating museum. Background information on this topic is found on the website of the R.J. and Diane Peterson Great Lakes Foundation and Keewatin Museum (*www.sskeewatin.com*).

4. The book *Place Names of Ontario* by Alan Rayburn, published by the University of Toronto Press in 1997, provided the main source of information for the backgrounds of these railway place names.

CHAPTER 2

1. *Colin Churcher's Railway Pages*, "The Bridges of Ottawa," *www.railways.incanada.net*.

2. "The Bridge Over the Ottawa River at Fitzroy," Colin Churcher and Raymond Farand, *Ottawa Central Railway Spareboard* (March 2008).

3. "The Canadian Northern Railway Bridge Over the South Nation River; or How Not to Build a Railway Bridge," Colin Churcher, *Branchline* (December 2008).

4. Investigations into the haunted bridges of the Hamilton area are published on the website *www.HamiltonParanormal.com*.

5. The account of the Desjardin Canal disaster is well-recounted by Alex and Judy Eberspaecher in "Desjardin Canal Railway Disaster," published in *Goodlife Magazine*, Vol. 10, Issue 8 (November 2008).

6. Metrolinx is an authority created by the Ontario government in 2006 to promote and coordinate transportation planning in the Greater Toronto Area. Its transportation plan, *The Big Move*, was published in 2008.

7. Author Michael Barnes has authored several volumes on the Ontario Northland Railway, in particular *Link With a Lonely Land*, (Erin, ON: Boston Mills Press, 1985), as well as *Ride the Polar Bear Express* (Burnstown, ON: General Store Publishing, 1996).

8. The Canadian lock is now a National Historic Site. Built in 1895, it completed the all-Canadian waterway through the Great Lakes and was the longest in the world at the time, and the first to use electrical power. Today, Parks Canada operates the canal for pleasure craft and the adjacent park contains many of the architecturally splendid red stone buildings that date

from the canal's construction and early operation. "Sault Ste. Marie Canal National Historic Site," Parks Canada website (*www.pc.gc.ca*).

CHAPTER 3

1. Ralph Benjamin Pratt, an architect and engineering draftsman from London, England, arrived in Canada in 1891 and joined the CPR in Winnipeg. In 1901, he began work with the Canadian Northern Railway designing stations until 1906, among his more spectacular being the CPR Virden station, and the CNo's Dauphin, Manitoba, station, as well as the magnificent Port Arthur station. He died in 1950. *The Manitoba Historical Society*, "Memorable Manitobans; Ralph Benjamin Pratt, 1872–1950," *www.mhs.mb.ca*.

2. One of the architectural "Holy Trinity" in the United States (which included Frank Lloyd Wright and Louis Sullivan), Henry Hobson Richardson travelled in 1860 to the Ecole des Beaux Arts in Paris, where he was deeply influenced by the Romanesque architecture of Spain and southern France. These influences, combined with his love for Byzantine architecture, led him to develop his unique style, which became known as "Richardsonian Romanesque," noted for its stonework and wide rounded arches. In addition to his notable church and library designs, he also designed a number of railway stations. His influence spread to other railway station architects, as reflected in station designs in Essex and Kingsville, Ontario. He died in 1886 at the age of forty-seven. Van Rensselaer. M.G. *Henry Hobson Richardson and His Works* (New York: Dover Publications, 1959).

CHAPTER 5

1. Anna Guérin's poppies soon became the international symbol of the Great War veterans across North America and in Europe. Tory Tronrud, "The Prince Arthur Hotel's Place in History," *Archives Association of Ontario, Conference, April 4, 2011* and *www.thegreatwar.co.uk/article/remembrance-poppy*.

2. Credit for the inside information on the Fairmont Château Laurier belongs to Deneen Perrin, director of public relations for the hotel.

3. According to author Terry Boyle, in his book *Marilyn at the French*, she may in fact still be there. Although she died in her Hollywood home, Boyle describes how visitors to the resort testify that they have seen the spectre of a beautiful blond woman in Cabin 15. Boyle, T. *Marilyn at French River and Other Ghostly Sightings* (Toronto: Polar Bear Press, 2003).

CHAPTER 6

1. Ron Brown. *Castles and Kings* (Toronto: Polar Bear Press, 2001) 168–171.

2. Ron Brown. "The Railway YMCAs", *The Train Doesn't Stop Here Anymore*, 3rd edition (Toronto: Dundurn, 2008) 132–133.

CHAPTER 7

1. The book *Engine Houses and Turntables in Canada 1850 to 1950* by E.F. Bush (Erin, ON: Boston Mills Press, 1999), remains the definitive work on this subject in Canada, and it is from this work that much of the historical information for this section is derived.

2. "Leaside Shops, Canadian National Railways," *Canadian Railway and Marine World* (March, 1921).

3. Dean Robinson. *Railway Stratford* (Erin, ON: Boston Mills Press, 1989). This work details the rise of Stratford's importance as a railway centre, as well as many of the personalities involved.

4. Douglas Smith, *A Century of Travel on the Ontario Northland Railway* (Ottawa: Trackside Canada, 2004).

CHAPTER 9

1. Kateri Tekakwitha, a Mohawk, was born in what is now New York State in 1656. Following the deaths of her parents, and scarred by smallpox, she was baptized by Jesuits in Montreal, who gave her the name Kateri (Mohawk for Catherine). She died in 1680 and is entombed in a shrine at St. Frances Xavier mission in Kahnawake, Quebec. The miracle that led to her canonization by Pope Benedict XVI in 2012 occurred in 2006 when the prayers of a six-year-old boy, dying from flesh-eating disease, to Kateri revived him from certain death. She is Canada's only Aboriginal saint and is known as the "Lily of the Mohawks." Eric Reguly, "In an Act of Atonement the Vatican Makes Kateri Tekakwitha the First Native Canadian Saint," *Globe and Mail*, Oct. 21, 2012.

2. Born in Hastings, England, Archibald Belaney, like many in England, was captivated by what was popularly termed the "red Indians." Upon his arrival in Canada in 1906, at age seventeen, Belaney made his way to Temagami where he joined with the local Bear Island band and began self-identifying as an Aboriginal named Grey Owl. Later, in Biscotasing on the CPR, he menaced the community with his knife and, in the face of possible arrest, fled town. As "Chief Grey Owl" he began lecturing and writing on the conservation of the Canadian Beaver, becoming an international celebrity. Following his death in Prince Albert, Saskatchewan, in 1938, where he had been serving as a park ranger, a North Bay newspaper revealed Grey Owl to be none other than the Englishman Belaney. Lovat Dickson. *Wilderness Man, the Strange Story of Grey Owl* (Scarborough: New American Library of Canada, 1973).

3. In early Ontario, shortlines were a common means of moving raw material to a particular industry or port. The Essex Terminal Railway and the Detroit River and Lake Erie Railway were early such examples. Eventually, the major railways took over most of these early lines. The modern era of shortlines began in Alberta in 1986 when the Central Western Railway took over the CNR's Stettler to Camrose subdivision. Today, large railway operators such as Rail America and Cando operate a number of Ontario's shortlines.

CHAPTER 11

1. Much of this information comes from the valuable research of, and personal communication with, George Bryant of Gravenhurst, and a visit to the site by the author.

BIBLIOGRAPHY

BOOKS AND ARTICLES

A Pictorial History of Algonquin Park. Toronto: Ontario Ministry of Natural Resources, 1977.

Andreae, Christopher. *Lines of Country: An Atlas of Railway and Waterway History in Canada*. Erin, ON: Boston Mills Press, 1997.

Barnes, Michael. *Link with a Lonely Land*. Erin, ON: Boston Mills Press, 1985.

_____. *Ride the Polar Bear Express*. Burnstown, ON: General Store Publishing, 1996.

Barr, Elinor. *Thunder Bay to Gunflint: The Port Arthur, Duluth, and Western Railway*. Thunder Bay, ON: The Thunder Bay Historical Museum Society, 1999.

Bell, Allan. *A Way to the West: A Canadian Railway Legend*. Barrie, ON: Privately published, 1991.

Boyle, T. *Marilyn at French River and Other Ghostly Sightings*. Toronto: Polar Bear Press, 2003.

Brampton Historical Society. "Brampton CPR Station." *Heritage Canada National Awards Nomination Submission, 2012.*

Brown, Ron. *Ghost Railways of Ontario*. Peterborough, ON: Broadview Press, 1989.

_____. *Ghost Railways of Ontario, Volume 2*. Toronto: Polar Bear Press, 2000.

_____. *The Train Doesn't Stop Here Anymore: An Illustrated History of the Railway Station in Canada*. Toronto: Dundurn, 2007).

Bush, E.F. *Engine Houses and Turntables in Canada 1850 to 1950*. Erin, ON: Boston Mills Press, 1999.

Churcher, Colin. "The 125th Anniversary of the Prince of Wales Bridge." *Branchline*, January 2006.

_____. "The Bridge over the Ottawa River at Fitzroy." *Ontario Central Railway Spareboard*, March 2008.

_____. "The Canadian Northern Bridge Over the South Nation, or How Not to Build a Railway Bridge." *Branchline*, December 2008.

_____. "The Centenary of the Interprovincial Bridge." *Branchline*, February 2001.

City of Thunder Bay, Heritage Registry. *Designated Property Number 2*, "CN Station," no date.

Coons, C.F. *The John R. Booth Story*. Ontario Ministry of Natural Resources, 1978.

Cooper, Charles. *Hamilton's Other Railway*. Ottawa: Bytown Railway Society, 2001.

_____. *Narrow Gauge for Us: The Story of the Toronto and Nipissing Railway*. Erin, ON: The Boston Mills Press, 1982.

Dickson, Lovat. *Wilderness Man: The Strange Story of Grey Owl*. Scarborough, ON: New American Library of Canada, 1973.

Eberspaecher, Alex and Judy. "The Desjardin Canal Railway Disaster." *Goodlife Magazine*, Vol. 10, Issue 8, November 2008.

Hansen, Keith. *Last Trains from Lindsay*. Roseneath, ON: Sandy Flats Publications, 2000.

Historic Sites and Monuments Board of Canada. *Railway Station Reports; RSR-19, Barrie (CNR), RSR-75, Palmerston (CNR), RSR-143, St. Mary's (CNR), RSR-171 North Bay (CNR), RSR-203 Orillia (CNR), RSR-232, Caledonia (CNR)*, various dates.

Jackson, John N. and John Burtniak. *Railways in the Niagara Peninsula*. Belleville, ON: Mika Publishing, 1981.

MacKay, Niall. *Over the Hills to Georgian Bay: A Pictorial History of the Ottawa, Arnprior, and Parry Sound Railway*. Erin, ON: Boston Mills Press, 1981.

Mackey, Doug. "Heritage Days Celebrate Brent's History." *Community Voices*, August 10, 2001.

"MacTier Celebrates a Century Thanks to the Tailway." *The Muskokan*, July 10, 2008.

Newell, Diane and Ralph Greenhill. *Survivals: Aspects of Industrial Archaeology in Ontario*. Erin, ON: Boston Mills Press, 1989.

Pitfield, Jane. *Leaside*. Toronto: Natural Heritage Books, 1999.

Plomer, James, with Alan R. Capon. *Desperate Venture: Central Ontario Railway*. Belleville, ON: Mika Publishing, 1979.

"Railfan Hotspots, Lake Superior North Shore." *Railfan*, Vol. 2, No. 3, Winter 2011.

Rayburn Alan. *Place Names of Ontario*. Toronto: University of Toronto Press, 1997.

Reguly, Eric. "In an Act of Atonement the Vatican Makes Kateri Tekakwitha the First Native Canadian Saint." *Globe and Mail*, October 21, 2012.

Robinson, Dean. *Railway Stratford*. Erin, ON: Boston Mills Press, 1989.

Robinson, Stephen and Tracie Steedhouse. "Grand Old Bridges." *The Grand River Watershed Bridge Inventory, Grand River Conservation Authority*, April 6, 2004.

Ross, Ian. "Mining May Breathe New Life into Thunder Bay Ore Dock." *Northern Ontario Business*, April 10, 2012.

Schuessler, Karl. *School on Wheels*. Erin, ON: Boston Mills Press, 1986.

Smith, Douglas N.W. *By Rail Road and Water to Gananoque*. Ottawa: Trackside Canada, 1995.

_____. *A Century of Travel on the Ontario Northland Railway*. Ottawa: Trackside Canada, 2004.

"Stiver Mill Restoration and Reuse, a Concept for Exploration." City of Markham, September 2010.

Tennant, Robert D. Jr. *Canada Southern Country*. Erin, ON: Boston Mills Press, 1991.

Van Rensselaer, M.G. *Henry Hobson Richardson and His Works*. New York: Dover Publications, 1959.

Wedlay, Brendan. "Quick Fix Urged for CP Railway Bridge Pedestrian Walkway." *Peterborough Examiner*, November 26, 2011.

Willmot, Elizabeth A. *Meet Me at the Station*. Toronto: Gage Publishing, 1976.

Wilson, Dale. *The Algoma Eastern Railway*. Sudbury, ON: Nickel Belt Rails, 1979.

Wilson, Donald M. *Lost Horizons: The Story of the Rathbun Company and the Bay of Quinte Railway*. Belleville, ON: Mika Publishing Company, 1983.

_____. *The Ontario and Quebec Railway*. Belleville, ON: Mika Publishing Company, 1984.

WEBSITES

"About Capreol: Northern Ontario Railroad Museum and Heritage Centre," *www.northernontariorail roadmuseum.ca*.

Agawa Canyon Tour Train, *www.agawacanyontourtrain.com*.

Alan Hilgendorf, Landscape Artist and Muralist, *www.hilgendorf.ca/bio.html*.

Architectural Conservatory of Ontario, Buildings at Risk, "MCR Rail Trestle Over Kettle Creek," *www.arconserv.ca/buildings_at_risk*.

"Brent Story," Algonquin Outfitters, *www.algonquinoutfitters.com*.

"Bridges Across the Don; Pottery Road to Riverdale," Points of Interest Along Lost Streams, *www.lostrivers.ca*.

"Bridges Over Niagara Falls, a History & Pictorial," *www.niagarafrontier.com/bridges.html*.

Brown, Edward, "A Walk Along the Don Valley Railway," *Torontoist*, September 29, 2010, *http://torontoist.com/2010/09/don_rail_branch_stays_gold*.

"Building Storeys, the Canadian Northern Railway's Eastern Lines Locomotive Shop," January 8, 2010, *Spacing Toronto* Online, *http://spacing.ca/toronto/2010/01/28*.

"Caledon Trailway," Ontario Rail Trails, *http://webhome.idirect.com/~brown/Caledon.html*.

"The Canada Atlantic Railway Research Site," *www.proto87.org/ca*.

Canada by Rail, *www.canadabyrail.ca*.

Canada Southern Railway, *www.canadasouthern.com/caso/home.htm*.

"Canada Southern Railway Station," St. Thomas, Ontario, the Railway Capital of Canada, *www.railwaycapital.ca/history_station*.

"Canadian Train Bridges and Trestles," *http//yourrailwaypictures.com/TrainBridges*.

"Cataraqui Trail," Ontario Rail Trails, *http://webhome.idirect.com/~brown/cataraqui.html*.

"Cataraqui Trail, Eastern Ontario's Path to Nature and History," *www.rideau-info.com/cattrail*.

Charles Cooper's Railway Pages, "Quick Railway Histories," *www.railwaypages.com*.

"Chrysler Canada Greenway," Essex Region Conservation Authority, *www.erca.org/conservation/area.chrylser_canada_greenway.cfm*.

Clarke, Rod, "Narrow Gauge Through the Bush," *www.narrowgaugethroughthebush.com*.

City of Markham, Markham Museum, "The Locust Hill Train Station," "The Acadia Train Car," *www.markham.ca*.

"Craigleith Station is now an Historic Heritage Museum," *www.model-railroad-info-guy/Craigleith-station.html*.

Doreton, Roger, "Major Canadian Bridge Projects of the 20th Century," History Notes, Special 2001 Edition of the Canadian Civil Engineer, *www.ryerson.ca*.

Elgin County Railway Museum, *www.ecrm5700.org*.

Elliot, Andrew, "The Train Stops Here: Washago is Still a Place Where Rail Passenger Adventures Begin," *Ramara Chronicle*, *www.ramarachronicle.com/feature.html*.

Essex Terminal Railway, *www.essexterminalrailway.com*.

"Exploring the K and P Trail," Mapsherpa, *www.mapsherpa.com/discover/mp*.

Farmer, Samuel, "The Coming of the Railway," Port Perry Scugog Township Heritage Gallery, *www.scugogheritage.com/history/agerailway.htm*.

Flack, Derek, "A Visual History of the Royal York Hotel," November 1, 2011, *www.blogto.com/city/2011/11/a_visual_history_of_the_royal_york_hotel*.

"Friendship Trail, Fort Erie," *www.friendshiptrail.ca*.

Glencoe and District Historical Society, "Glencoe Train Station," *www.glencoehistoricalsociety.ca*.

"Grand Junction Railway," *www.vishwawalking.ca/grand-junction-rr*.

"Grand River Railway," *www.trainweb.org/elso/grr.htm*.

"Hamilton Brantford Cambridge Trails," Ontario Rail Trails, *http://webhome.idirect.com/-brown/hamilton_cambridge.htm*.

Harwood Station Museum, *www.harwoodmuseum.ca*.

"The Haunting of the Sydenham Road Railway Bridge," Hamilton Paranormal, *http//hamiltonparanormal.com/bridges1.html*.

Heritage Bridges of Ontario, *www.heritagebridges.org*.

Historic Rail Tour of the Barrie-Allandale Rail Facilities, *www.model-railroad-infoguy.com*.

Historic Sites and Monuments Board of Canada, "Railway Station Reports," *http//cn-in-ontario.com/Reports/index*.

"History of the Line," *www.ydhr.on.ca/HistoryOfTheLine.html*.

"History of Parry Sound," *www.zeuter.com/parrysd/history.htm*.

"History of the Port Perry Grain Elevator," *www.scugogheritage.com/history/grainelevator.htm*.

"The Hogg's Bay Trestle," Township of Tay, *www.tay.ca/Community/History/TheHoggsBayTrestle/index.htm*.

The Huntsville and Lake of Bays Railway, *www.portageflyer.org*.

The Huntsville Train Station Society, *www.huntsvilletrainstation.com*.

"John Rudolphus Booth, Lumber King and Entrepreneur," Trinity Western University, *http://twu.ca/sites/laurentian/heritage/jrbooth.html*.

"The K and P Trail, a New Use for an Abandoned Railway," *http://post.queensu.ca/-ab25/kandptrail/Dillon.htm*.

"The K and P Trail," *www.cityofkingston/pdf/maps/K&P_Trail-parking.pdf*.

Kennedy, Raymond L., "Toronto Suburban Railway, Guelph Radial Line," Old Time Trains, *www.trainweb.net*.

Lake Erie and Northern Railway, *http://trainweb/elso/len.htm*.

"Lower Trent Trail," Vishwawalking, *http://vishwawalking.ca/hastings-heritage-trail/lower-trent-trail.html.*

Lynn Valley Trail, *www.lynnvalleytrail.ca.*

MacDonald, Mady, "Hiking the Dundas Valley," *www.out-there.com/dundas.htm.*

Don Makela, Artist, *http://donmakela.com/mural/menu.htm.*

"MCR Railway Trestle over Kettle Creek," Architecture Conservancy of Ontario, Buildings at Risk, *www.arconserv.ca/buildings_at_risk.*

Memory Junction Museum, *http//brightonrailwaymuseum.homestead.com.*

Mimico Station Community Organization, "Station History," *http://mimicostation.ca.*

"Mural Map of Canada," Mural Routes, *www.muralroutes.com.*

Muskoka Rails Museum, *www.muskokaraiolsmuseum.com.*

"Niagara Falls Railroads, a History," *www.niagarafallsfrontier.com/railroadhistory.html#82.*

"Niagara Rails-CN Lines," *http://home.cogeco.ca/~trains/rrcn.htm.*

Niagara Railway Museum, *www.nfrm.ca.*

"North Simcoe Rail Trail," *www.simcoecountytrails.net/nsrt.htm.*

Northern Ontario Railroad Museum and Heritage Centre, *http://normhc.ca/silverstripe.*

"The Old K and P Roadbed," Renfrew County and District Health Unit, *www.rcdhu.com/health-info/activity/walk-kandp.htm.*

Ontario Heritage Trust, "North Bay CPR Station (North Bay), 1903," *www.heritagetrust.on.ca.*

Ontario Heritage Trust, "Owen Sound CPR Station, Baseline Documentation Report," July 2010, *www.owensound.ca/documents/Oct_10_CPR_baseline_report.htm.*

"Ontario Murals on Buildings," *www.dalejtravis.com/barnpic/picbldg/on.htm.*

Ontario Southland Railway Inc., *www.osrinc.ca.*

"Our Past, Ottawa and New York Railway Bridge," Cornwall, Ontario, *www.ourhometown.ca.*

Palmerston Heritage Railway Museum, *www.palmerstonrailwaymuseum.com.*

Petrov, Tom, "Travelling the Abandoned Railways of Ontario," *www.tompetrovphotography/abandonedrailway page4.html.*

"A Photo Gallery of Grain Elevators in Ontario," *www.grainelevators.ca.*

"Pontypool Grain Elevator," Ontario's Abandoned Places, *www.ontarioabandonedplaces.com.*

"Port Dover and Lake Huron Railway Company," *www.stocklobster.com/podolahuraco.html.*

"Rail Trails for Hiking," Hike Ontario Fact Sheet 9, *www.hikeontario.com/bulletin/factsheets.*

Railway Depot Museums, *www.rshs.org/depotmuseums.*

"Railway Stations of Ontario," compiled by Rob Hughes, *www.trainweb.org/ontariostations/index.htm.*

Railways of Eastern Ontario, *www.railwaybob.cam.*

"Railways of Ontario," Ontario Railway History Page, *www.trainweb.org/ontariorailways/.*

Railways of Ottawa, *www.railways.incanada.net.*

"Riding the Ottawa Carleton Trailway, Ottawa to Carleton Place," *www.GoBiking.ca*

Robinson, Jamie, "Bike Back in Time on the Tay Shore Trail," *Toronto Star*, July 6, 2009, *www.thestar.com/travel/article/660001.*

"Rose Point Recreational Trail," *www.twp.seguin.on.ca/975/rose-point-recreational-trail.htm.*

Rotary Club of Stirling, *www.stirlingrotary.ca*, background to the railway station project,

"Roundhouse Park," Toronto Railway Historical Association, *www.trha/roundhousepark.html.*

"Royal York Hotel," A View on Cities, *www.aviewoncities.com/toronto/royalyorkhotel.htm.*

Saugeen Rail Trail, *www.saugeenrailtrail.com.*

"SC Johnson Paris to Brantford Trail," Grand River Trails, *www.grandriver.ca.*

Scrimgeour, Pat, "Historical Outline of Railways in Southwestern Ontario," UCRS Newsletter, July 1990, *www.railwaypages.com.*

Schabas, Jake, "Throwback Thursday, The Belt Line Railway," *Spacing Toronto*, July 16, 2009, *http://spacingtoronto.ca.*

"Self Guided Walking Tours of Carleton Place," *http://carletonplace.*

"Significant Dates in Ottawa Railway History," Colin Church's Railway Pages, *www.railwaysincanada.net.*

Smith, Mary, "Historical Background of the Grand Trunk Railway," St. Mary's Museum, *http://stonetown.com/gttsm/history.htm.*

"Smiths Falls Bascule Bridge," *http://wikimapia.org/10236138/Smiths-Falls-Bascule-Bridge.*

"The Story of the Canadian Pacific Railway," *www.cpr.ca/en/about-cp/our-past-present-and-future/Documents/cp-childrens-history.pdf.*

"Stratford Ontario Acquires CNR Shops for Redevelopment," Toronto Railway Historical Association, November 11, 2010, *www.trha.ca/2010/2/stratford-ontario-acquires-cnr-shops.html.*

"Stratford's Railway Industry," *www.welcometoStratford.com/media/pdf/railwayindustry.pdf.*

"Surviving Steam Locomotives in Canada," *www.steamlocomotive.com.*

"Tay Shore Trail," Simcoe County Trails, *www.simcoecountytrails.net.*

"Tiny Trail," Simcoe County Trails, *www.simcoecountytrails.net.*

Thornton-Cookstown Trans Canada Trail, *www.simcoetrails.net/tctrail.htm.*

"To the Mettawas," *Walkerville Times*, *www.walkervilletimes.com/26/to-the-mettawas.html*.

The Toronto Hamilton and Buffalo Railway Society, *www.thbrailway.ca*.

"Toronto's Railway Legacy Begins in 1853," Toronto Railway Historical Association, *www.trha.ca/history. html*.

Trillium Railway, *www.trilliumrailway.com*.

"The Unofficial Website of the Algoma Eastern Railway," *www.magma.ca*.

"The Victoria County Recreation Corridor," *www.kawartha.net*.

"Victoria Recreation Transportation Corridor & Haliburton County Rail Trail," *www.webhome.idirect. com/~brown/victoria.htm*.

"A Visual History of the Royal York Hotel," *http//bogto.com/city/2011/11/a_visual_history_of_the_royal_ york_hotel*.

Waterloo Central Railway, *www.waterloocentralrailway.com*.

Waterloo Region Museum, *www.waterlooregionmuseum.com*.

Zandbergen, Lewis, "An Historical Summary of the Stirling Grand Trunk/CN Railway Station," the Rotary Club of Stirling, *www.rotarystirling.ca/history_trainstation.html*.

Note: All websites were active as of November 2012.

RAILWAY ABBREVIATIONS

ACR, Algoma Central Railway

B&LH, Buffalo and Lake Huron Railway

B&O, Brampton and Orangeville Railway

BB&G, Buffalo Brantford and Goderich Railway

Bcr, Barrie Collingwood Railway

BQR or **BOQ**, Bay of Quinte Railway

CASO, Canada Southern Railway

CN Rail, **CNR**, Canadian National Railways

CNo, Canadian Northern Railway

COR, Central Ontario Railway

ETR, Essex Terminal Railway

GJR, Grand Junction Railway

GT, Grand Trunk Railway

GWR, Great Western Railway

H&NW, Hamilton and Northwestern Railway

IB&O, Irondale Bancroft and Ottawa Railway

LE&DR, Lake Erie and Detroit River Railway

MCR, Michigan Central Railway

N&NW, Northern and Northwestern Railway

NTR, National Transcontinental Railway

ONR, Ontario Northland Railway

OS&H, Ontario Simcoe and Huron Railway

SSR, South Simcoe Railway

T&NO, Temiskaming and Northern Ontario Railway

TG&B, Toronto, Grey and Bruce Railway

TH&B, Toronto, Hamilton and Buffalo Railway

TIR, Thousand Islands Railway

WG&B, Wellington, Grey and Bruce Railway

Y&D, York and Durham Heritage Railway

INDEX

PLACES, MUSEUMS, AND TOUR TRAINS

BY THE SAME AUTHOR

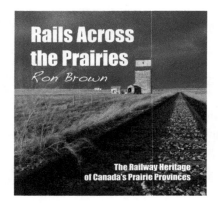

Rails Across the Prairies
The Railway Heritage of Canada's Prairie Provinces
by Ron Brown
978-1459702158
$29.99

Rails Across the Prairies traces the evolution of Canada's rail network, including the appearance of the first steam engine on the back of a barge. The book looks at the arrival of European settlers before the railway and examines how they coped by using ferry services on the Assiniboine and North Saskatchewan Rivers. The work then follows the building of the railways, the rivalries of their owners, and the unusual irrigation works of Canadian Pacific Railway. The towns were nearly all the creation of the railways from their layout to their often unusual names.

Eventually, the rail lines declined, though many are experiencing a limited revival. Learn what the heritage lover can still see of the Prairies' railway legacy, including existing rail operations and the stories the railways brought with them. Many landmarks lie vacant, including ghost towns and elevators, while many others survive as museums or interpretative sites.

VISIT US AT
Dundurn.com
@dundurnpress
Facebook.com/dundurnpress
Pinterest.com/dundurnpress